The Wonderful World of
STEAM
Locomotives

The Wonderful World of STEAM LOCOMOTIVES

P. B. Whitehouse

Hamlyn
London · New York · Sydney · Toronto

Acknowledgements

The publishers are grateful to the following for the illustrations reproduced in this book:
P. M. Alexander; D. Cross; Frank Dumbleton; Harold Edmundson; T. H. Gilderslieve; E. J.
Gulash; J. B. Hollingsworth; P. J. Howard; P. J. Huntingdon; A. J. Lambert; E. Lambert; R.
Lush; J. Marsh; Colin Miell; D. Rodgers; D. T. Rowe; J. B. Snell; Brian Stephenson; N.
Tate; Tore Westerman; Colin White; C. M. Whitehouse; P. B. Whitehouse; J. S. Whiteley.

Paintings: Jim Petrie (John Adam's collection); F. Moore (Rixon Bucknall's collection); C.
Hamilton Ellis (Lord Garnock's collection); Colourviews Picture Library.

This book was produced for The Hamlyn Publishing Group by
Colourviews Publications.

Published by The Hamlyn Publishing Group Limited
London · New York · Sydney · Toronto
Astronaut House, Feltham, Middlesex, England
Copyright © The Hamlyn Publishing Group Limited 1978

ISBN 0 600 38268 0

Filmset in Great Britain by Photocomp Limited, Birmingham
Reproductions by Metric Reproductions Limited, Chelmsford, Essex
Printed and bound in Spain by Mateu Cromo Artes Graficas SA,
Madrid

Contents

The Glorious Years

From the middle of the nineteenth to the middle of the twentieth centuries steam locomotives hauled most of the world's trains. A journey by that *train-de-luxe* popularly known as the *Orient Express* from Paris to Instanbul, for example, once involved more than twenty changes of steam engine, although this was well before the introduction of diesel and electric traction and of the train's demise in 1977.

Some 500,000 working steam locomotives provided the world with transport during that century of glorious years and even today some 25,000 are still at work. The decline in numbers has enhanced the love which many men feel for this most fascinating of machines – a fact which is born out by the enormous crowds that turn out to see or travel on special steam trains in countries where they have been superseded.

In its heyday, however, it was within everyone's reach and one cannot help but envy the opportunities which came to one of Britain's better known railway travellers, T. R. Perkins. His ambition, which he achieved before the end of a long life, was to travel over every stretch of railway open to passengers in the British Isles. At the beginning of this century that was an extremely formidable task.

Fortunately, T.R.P., as he was known to many, kept a diary and was able to tell the story of some of his adventures, particularly in the pages of the famous monthly journal, *The Railway Magazine*. His overall journeys from Warwick involved travelling behind classic steam locomotives of the period, most of them with inside cylinders and with only four coupled wheels. In those days it was the rule rather than the exception that superb cleanliness was the order of things and Perkins must have seen some magnificent sights, with locomotives and coaches in every hue. With hindsight, one realises that he must have encountered a remarkable cross-section of British motive power.

Warwick was on the Great Western's main line, on which he would see dark green express engines adorned with polished brass and copper. At that time this company's locomotives normally had double frames and coupled driving wheels, although this was still the era of the graceful single-wheeler. From Warwick the next step was to Rugby, one of the hubs of one of the largest of Britain's railways, the London & North Western,

busy with blackberry-black engines with cast brass number plates, evocative names and shrill, high-pitched whistles. The company was then at the end of an era dominated by its dictatorial Chief Mechanical Engineer, Francis Webb, whose Crewe works had produced magnificent simple 2-4-0s for express passenger working plus a variety of not so good compounds, ranging from 2-2-0s through 2-2-2-2s to 4-4-0s.

Leaving the LNWR Perkins crossed the town to its second station and a completely different scene. Here the Great Central, proud of its new and costly stretch of railway from Sheffield to the heart of London, used its latest inside-cylindered 4-4-0s – the traditional British express design and one which was to continue being built for the next decade.

Reaching Sheffield, T.R.P. rode across country to Hull and en route he saw the Midland Railway, with its gleaming red engines (also with inside cylinders), maybe travelling behind one of the Kirtley double-framed 2-4-0s. Part of the journey was over the erstwhile Hull and Barnsley Railway, where large domeless 4-4-0s designed by Matthew Stirling, son of the famous Patrick Stirling of the Great Northern Railway, headed the faster trains.

Moving on, the next great railway was the North Eastern, whose main line provided an important section of the East Coast route from London to Scotland. The journey was via Yarm, the birthplace of the Stockton and Darlington Railway Company – the first public steam railway, dating from 1825. The North Eastern had light green engines and also used 2-4-0s and 4-4-0s in general service, the latter with well-enclosed cabs, which were unusual for this period.

Travelling across the country again, Perkins took the North Eastern's Wensleydale branch through Bedale to Hawes Junction, later Garsdale, on the Midland Railway's new main line, built to provide that company with the much sought after route of its own from London to Scotland. His return home involved as many as ten more changes of train and again the motive power was of classic design in the form of gleaming 2-4-0s and 4-4-0s.

As he exhausted opportunities nearer at hand, so Perkins extended his travels, going north to Scotland, where the Caledonian, North British, Glasgow and South Western, Highland and Great North of Scotland railways covered the country, with

Whilst Britain and Europe still used miniscule engines with only one pair of driving wheels the railroads of North America, busily opening up the continent, had 4-4-0s, vestibuled coaches and bogie freight cars. They were helping to build a nation

Red was the colour chosen by Britain's Midland Railway by the beginning of the twentieth century. Superb cleanliness was the order of the day and most engines were of neat inside-cylindered design, some, like this Kirtley 2-4-0, with double frames

9

locomotives in blue, brown, green, yellow and black respectively. Perhaps the greatest company meeting place of all was Carlisle Citadel Station, the gateway to Scotland via the West Coast and Midland routes.

Locomotive design moved into its next stage as the years rolled on toward the First World War, heavier trains demanding more powerful locomotives. The 2-4-0 was at the end of its main-line life and the 4-4-0 in its heyday, with the 4-6-0 slowly gaining precedence. During the later days of the period the zenith of the inside-cylindered locomotive design was reached with such examples as the LNWR *George the Fifth* 4-4-0s and the Caledonian *Dunalastairs*. Carlisle regularly saw such glamorous locomotives as the Caledonian's famous Cardean 4-6-0 in blue lined out in white; the North Western *Precursor* 4-4-0s and *Experiment* 4-6-0s; the Midland's red 700 Class with Belpaire fireboxes and even some of the new three-cylinder compound 4-4-0s which would become famous; North Eastern 4-4-0s in light green and Glasgow and South Western 4-6-0s in dark green.

The great West Coast alliances of the time were between the North Western and the Caledonian on one hand and the Midland with the Glasgow and South Western on the other. Each alliance was competing for passengers between London and Glasgow.

Progress was equally swift on the East Coast line, with the Great Northern, North Eastern and North British working together to carry traffic between London and Edinburgh. Atlantic type 4-4-2s were prominent on each section of the journey to Edinburgh (the West Coast alliance never took to this type).

It was, however, left to the Great Western Railway, with main lines from London to the South West and North West, to make the real locomotive advances during this period. The great leap forward was made by GWR Chief Mechanical Engineer, G.J. Churchward, who was wise enough to look for the best elsewhere and combine it with his own ideas and good British practice. He took a hard look at contemporary locomotives in America and copied many features; he also imported three of the famous de Glehn compounds based on the designs of the Northern Railway of France. These he put to extended trials alongside his own new 4-4-2s and 4-6-0s. The complications of the compounds ruled them out and Churchward's own two-cylinder *Saints* and four-cylinder *Star* 4-6-0s emerged as standard for the GWR. The *Saint* design was later modified to emerge as the mixed traffic *Hall* class and the *Stars* were 'stretched' into the great *Castles* and *Kings,* which ruled on the Western until the end of steam. These designs exerted considerable influence on British locomotive practice generally.

In the South three main lines served the ports and the South West. The South Eastern & Chatham ran the boat trains to Dover and Folkestone behind their D and E class 4-4-0s, later to be rebuilt as some of the finest examples of the type in the country, whilst the London Brighton & South Coast Railway also ran to the Channel port of Newhaven using 4-4-0s and Atlantics. The LBSC's crack train was all-Pullman to Brighton, later known as the Southern

Belle, its motive power the then huge
umber-painted 4-6-4 and 4-6-2 tanks.

The last but certainly not the least
of the lines in the South was the
London & South Western, which
competed with the Great Western for
traffic to Plymouth and the South
West as well as serving the South
Coast from Portsmouth to Exeter.
The star LSWR engines of the period
were 4-4-0s, led by Dugald Drummond's exemplary T9 class.

During this period there were
various unofficial railway races. Late
in the nineteenth century there had
been open competition to Scotland
over the East and West Coast routes,
in 1895 for example such magnificent
machines as the LNWR's record
breaking Precedent class 2-4-0 *Hard-
wicke* and the Great Northern's Stirling Single No. 1, plus, of course, that
graceful machine built as an exhibition piece by Neilsons and acquired
by the Caledonian Railway, single
wheeler No 123. The race for the
Ocean Mails, on the other hand, was
between the Great Western and the
London & South Western Railway
to acquire the right to carry these
from Plymouth to London.

During those halcyon years amateur enthusism for railways was a very
British pastime, but the British mag-
azines reported development on railways in other countries. In Europe it
is probably true to say that Germany
exerted the most influence over
locomotive design, while France
achieved greater technical advances.
From a race of individualists such as
the French it was inevitable that their
products would not only appear
unique but also be physically like no
others. It is safe to say that the French
could have taught the world a great
deal about steam locomotives – particularly concerning the art of com-
pounding – had the world been prepared to listen. German engines were
also the result of a distinctive school
of design. Their symmetrical shape
seemed to carry the external plumb-
ing more harmoniously than French
locomotives.

The Germans and Austrians made
considerable progress in exporting
their designs to Central Europe. To
the British traveller it was, perhaps, a
little confusing, for the colours of the
engines were generally drab and all
the festooned locomotives looked

horribly alike to unaccustomed eyes. It is worth remembering, however, that it was in the Edwardian era that such great exporting firms as Henschel and Krupp began work in earnest to supply the needs of Central Europe and Turkey, and later to share with Britain her imperial locomotive market.

The American scene was even wider for it was the railroads that had opened up the country westwards and, over a considerable area, preceded settlement. By the turn of the century there were nearly 200,000 miles of track administered by hundreds of companies, big and small. There could be no man such as Perkins able to travel or even know them all. Because of the speed of expansion and consequent need for traction power, giant private locomotive works flourished in America. The best known were Baldwin, Alco (the American Locomotive Company) and Lima, each competing for business at home and, before long, the world over. American locomotive practice thus had an influence in the coming railways of all the Colonial powers and, naturally, on the newly founded freedom states of South America.

The early years of the twentieth century saw considerable expansion in the United States and in 1905 no less than 6,000 new locomotives were ordered from these now big companies. Contrary to British and European practice, American engines tended to be constructed to work hard with a short life in view. By European standards they were rough and ready and only to be imported when domestic locomotive building was overloaded! Nevertheless, American practice was not to be ignored and even Britain learned from it.

Looking back, it can be said that the finest years of steam began when the infant had become a child and ended with the First World War, when the child had achieved maturity. Britain and the major European countries had overseas possessions which were developing and private locomotive builders such as Beyer Peacock, North British, Vulcan and Robert Stephenson joined in the race for the markets of the world. Rail transport was then still the only conceivable method of moving passengers and freight in bulk at reasonable cost and reasonable speed. Another World War was to change the face of things to come far beyond man's dreams or fears. Amongst these changes came the end of steam's ascendancy and, alas, of the glorious years.

The London & South Western Railway competed with the Great Western for the traffic from the ocean terminal at Plymouth to London. Its other main line from the channel port of Weymouth, via Bournemouth was a popular holiday route. These green 4-6-0s of Drummond design were nicknamed *Paddleboxes* because of their huge splashers

Steam Safari

If Britain's T.R. Perkins was the first of the Determined Travellers, an American, Rogers Whitaker, is probably the greatest: at the time of writing his rail journeyings add up to 2,451,903 miles. Whitaker made his first railway journey in a slip coach of the Great Western Railway out of Paddington station, London, in 1902, as a babe in arms. In May 1977 he wrote that during that year alone he had already had the good fortune to travel nearly 5,000 miles *by steam*.

Whilst one can only dream of some of the wonders of steam which Rogers Whitaker has seen, smelled and travelled behind, those of us who have had the good fortune to travel the world on a lesser scale, either voluntarily for pleasure of for some business reason, or compulsorily by direction of the military, can at least share some of his memories. Perhaps a few have ridden on trains that he has missed, for like Perkins, Whitaker set himself a target of travelling over every mile of railway in his native land; the World came later.

The author well remembers Second World War trips over Canadian rails to flying stations, journeys on leave spent in the USA and later the railways of North, East and West Africa and of India. In those days it was steam all the way. For some, it was not pleasant: the Japanese, for example, used prisoners of war to build new lines in their areas of control, and the story of these railways of death is grim.

The first journeys over Canadian railroads were full of fascination. There were the huge 4-8-4s and 4-8-2s of the Canadian National, with

trains of comfortable dark green coaches and dining cars which supplied meals undreamed of in rationed Britain. The engines in the Hamilton area provided considerable variety in classes and types and they covered at least four railroads. The New York Central ran in, using the famous *Hudson* type 4-6-4s, the Canadian Pacific with light 4-6-2s on Hamilton-Toronto fasts and ugly streamlined 4-4-4s for branch work. Lastly there was the Toronto, Hamilton & Buffalo, a joint line which had its own 2-8-4s for freight.

No 7029 *Clun Castle*, now privately preserved, hauls steam passenger trains over British Railway's tracks between Birmingham, Oxford and Didcot on special excursions, from time to time

Africa provided more than a glimpse of steam, mostly on the Egyptian State Railways but East and West Africa also had their moments of interest. In northern Africa the easier terrain of the flatter coastal areas allowed speeds considerably in excess of those of the south and the railways were mostly standard gauge, rather than metre or 3 ft 6 in, the standard 'African' gauge. Some of these northern lines were highly utilised; for example, in Algeria, theoretically part of Metropolitan France, there were 4-6-2 + 2-6-4 Garratts capable of 80 mph, and the equally famous Egyptian State Railways' Atlantics. The ESR tended, somewhat naturally, to concentrate on lower Egypt, with main lines between Cairo and Alexandria and Cairo and Port Said via Ismalia. There were also intensive suburban services operating out of Cairo and Alexandria. Even as late as 1955 the ESR owned nearly 800 steam locomotives, and Cairo station was a real enthusiasts' paradise.

While the motive power was of fascinating variety, in the form of 4-4-0s, 4-6-0s, 2-8-0s of First World War period and ancient double-framed 0-6-0s, the main express power was the 4-4-2 Atlantic. These engines in well cleaned green livery were the backbone of the ESR express engine rosters for more than 40 years; the pioneers of 1905, incidentally, were de Glehn compounds. The

most exacting duties occurred on the Cairo to Alexandria expresses, with their luxurious white-painted carriages, including Pullman cars operated by the Compagnie Internationale des Wagons-Lits. The journey time for the 130 miles was two-and-a-half hours and this required speeds of up to 75 mph. The star of the fleet was a superbly decorated engine kept at Cairo main shed – King Farouk's royal engine; others carried the names of ancient Egyptian kings, including *Rameses II, Thotmes III, Amenhotep* and the memorable *Ibrahim Pasha*. Fortunately, when steam finished in 1963 one of these flyers was preserved and is in Cairo's Railway Museum.

The last summers of steam came and went in the 1950s and 1960s. In North America the diesel had already taken hold. The March of General Motors was to end in victory at the beginning of the period – it did not take long for the railroads of the USA and Canada to change completely to the internal-combustion engine and the familiar wail of the steam whistle at the grade crossings became a memory. Gone were New York Central's Hudsons, the Big Boys of the Union Pacific and the Selkirks of the Canadian Pacific; the steam engine became a museum piece. This did not deter the Whitakers of this world, whose ambition to travel over tracks before they disappeared and

above
Canadian National Railway used 4-8-4s and 4-8-2s for its main line passenger trains and today one of them can still be seen at the head of regular excursions from Toronto to Niagara Falls. Here, in 1958 at Guelph, Ontario, a 4-6-2 heads a 4-8-4 with a special excursion.

above, right
The diesel had already taken a firm hold in the USA by the 1950s but some steam was kept for the rail fan. Here, in April 1969, Richard Jensen's ex Grand Trunk Western No 5629 takes a trip to Port Huron

right
One of the most modern steam engines to survive the holocaust is Union Pacific 4-8-4 No 8444. This superb locomotive is still used to haul UP's colourful yellow coaches on fan trips.

while travel was still possible remained as difficult as that of the steam enthusiast seeking out locomotives before *they* disappeared from the railway scene.

An enthusiast's paradise in the 1950s was Ireland. During those days of tranquility the old Great Southern Company had become state-owned Coras Iompair Eirean and the Northern Counties Committee of the LMS, the railway section of the Ulster Transport Authority, but the Great Northern of Ireland was still independent, with over 800 miles of track. One could travel on the GN's *Enterprise* express between Dublin and Belfast behind Glover's large-boilered 4-4-0 simples and compounds with names like *Eagle* and *Falcon*, *Peregrine* and *Kestrel*.

The Great Northern, the second largest railway system in Ireland, soon to go into insolvency because of partition, painted its passenger engines in sky-blue and scarlet and most carried names: *Slieve*, *Gullion* and *Lugnaquilla*, *Galtee More* and *Croagh Patrick* headed clerestory-roofed coaches of teak and the *Bundoran Express* left Dublin for the west daily.

Not that the other big companies lacked interest – far from it. Very Victorian-looking 4-4-0s still worked the stoppers and branch trains in the North and the giant 4-6-0 *Maeve*, with her sister engines, heaved the Dublin mails up the steep grades from

right
Ireland possessed some charming rural lines during the 1950s, including the CIE branch to Loughrea. Most were worked by ancient 0-6-0 tanks, but here an old Great Southern 2-4-0 was the regular engine

below
The Great Northern Railway of Ireland was to go into insolvency and nationalisation during the 1950s. Its main line from Dublin to Belfast still exists but gone are the fine 4-4-0s clad in sky blue and scarlet

below, right
Some of the finest steam locomotive work in Europe during the late 1950s and early 1960s was done in France. This was particularly so over the route of the *Fleche d'Or*, using 231K Pacifics between Calais and Amiens

Cork station, 1 in 78 steepening to 1 in 60 for two miles. It was Irish mainline steam at its best. Branch lines had ancient 2-4-0s, 0-6-0s and all manner of tank engines which trundled venerable six-wheeled coaches over grass-grown tracks. All in all, variety was the essence of the Irish railway scene. Later in the decade O.V.S. Bulleid came to the CIE's Inchicore works as Chief Mechanical Engineer to introduce diesel, but not before trying out something typically Irish: a turf-burning steam engine. Bulleid, one of the last apostles of steam, was anything less than a tryer and some would say he was a leader in his field.

Some of the finest steam locomotive work in Europe during this period was in France, particularly over the northern section of SNCF from Calais to Paris and on the roads west from Le Mans to Brest and to the south, over the tracks of the old PLM. There were journeys to remember: the Night Ferry Sleeper over the English Channel or the Golden Arrow service – each had its peculiar attractions and each train into France would be headed by world-famous compound Pacifics, usually K class but if one was lucky, a Chapelon 231 E.

To the logical French, a machine is something to be studied and this approach was applied to their steam as well as their diesel and electric locomotives. Their drivers were and still are taught in considerable detail exactly how a locomotive works and how to get the best performance from it. In steam days a crew gained a bonus for fuel economy but an even larger one was offered for punctuality and recovering time lost for reasons 'beyond their control.' Yet lost time recovery was itself controlled by means of a recording speedometer which indicated any breach of restriction or operating procedure; disciplinary action followed. In such ways French steam railway operation followed a consistent pattern of orderliness and was able to achieve reliability and precision.

The laurels for the most efficient and impressive passenger engine class ever to run in Europe went, without doubt, to the 35 241P class compound 4-8-2s based on a PLM design but built by the SNCF after 1947. These examples of Chapelon's skill were still employed well into the 1960s. One route they worked was to the Massif Central via Clermont Ferrand, following the Loire through Bourges

above, left
Perhaps the laurels of French steam went
to Chapelon's mighty SNCF 241P
Mountains on the Paris–Brest and
Paris–Clermont Ferrand runs. These
compound 4-8-2s based on a PLM design
were amongst the most efficient and
impressive engines to be seen in the latter
days of steam

left
France's most prolific class in post Second
World War days was the 141R imported
from the New World to fill a gap caused
by hostilities. These USA and Canadian
built engines existed in both coal and oil
burning versions and proved to be the
last steamers to run in France in regular
service

above
Germany, too, had some superb power
and in later years the fine 01 class Pacifics
attracted many steam enthusiasts

and Saincaze, Moulins and the sleepy
junction of St Germain-des-Fosses to
Nevers where engines changed. The
deafening sound of one of the mon-
sters climbing with a Rapide loaded
with up to 13 coaches was not one
easily forgotten.

Germany, too, had some fine
power, which in the form of its 01
and 03 Pacifics, lasted well into the
1970s. The Pacific tradition is a long
one in Germany and perhaps the
most celebrated of all were the
elegant old Bavarian Maffei compounds. Of late the standard Reichsbahn 01s made headlines in the Press,
with train after train being timed and
photographed by rail fans, especially
on the heavily-graded route to Hof.
Today these engines are silent in the
Federal Republic but those who

travel east know that the Deutsche
Reichbahn still makes good use of
their services; the sight is well worth
the tiresome formalities of the border
crossing.

Australia and New Zealand dispensed with the use of regular steam
comparatively early. The former had
lines of several gauges, varying from
3 ft 6 in through standard up to 5 ft
3 in, and used large engines, including
Pacifics and 4-8-2s for their passenger
services, and Garratts. By the mid-
1960s main-line steam was gone for
all practical purposes, including the
magnificent class 500 4-8-2s which
ran on the South Australian 5 ft 3 in
gauge, taking 500-ton trains over the
Mount Lofty Range. There were also
some later 4-8-4s of class 520 which
carried a streamlined casing similar to

above
With steam disappearing fast in West Germany many rail fans looked further east for their hobby. East German steam locomotives such as this glistening Pacific still crossed the border to Hamburg whenever they worked the expresses from Berlin. The morning express is seen here leaving Hamburg on the return journey

left
Austria still operates a few main-line steam engines; for many years most of these have been ex-German Reichsbahn *Kriegslok* austerity 2-10-0s fitted with an Austrian invention – the Giesl ejector intended to improve their efficiency when burning poor-quality coal

right
South Australia uses the 5 ft 3 in gauge and its steam power included the massive 500 and 520 class Pacifics. The latter were streamlined and so successful were they that No 520 herself has been kept in preservation, running steam specials for rail fans

The Western Australia Railway is built to the 3 ft 6 in gauge but nonetheless used large motive power. This Robert Stephenson & Hawthorn class V 2-8-2 at Midlands Junction, Perth in 1970, was built as late as 1955

those Pennsylvanian PR giants, the T1 class 4-4-4-4 Duplex engines. The 520s were almost 100 per cent passenger engines and one has been kept running as a 'live' museum exhibit.

After a false start with the standard gauge, New Zealand adopted 3 ft 6 in as being more suitable for a sparsely inhabited pastoral country. In later days the handsome J class 4-8-2s and K class 4-8-4s handled most of the traffic, along with a few older class Ab Pacifics. To see the Js and Ks hard at work was to see New Zealand steam at its peak.

The country had one of the most dramatic inclines used for passenger working in the world, the famous 1 in 15 Rimutuka incline between Masterton and Wellington in North Island. Here for 77 years the little Fell engines, using their horizontal driv-

ing wheels to grip the central rail, thundered their way – sometimes five to a train – up the hill from Cross Creek. In 1955 the incline was superseded by a tunnel.

By the 1960s steam was becoming ever more elusive. In Britain it was soon to vanish and the first railway region to go completely diesel was the Western, at the close of 1965. Elsewhere steam lingered on, finally to come to an end in August 1968. Even in those last years there was still the occasional 'steam spectacular' to be found, usually promoting an enthusiasts' event. An example was the co-operation of enthusiasts and the Western Region in May 1964, culminating in the running of the very last high-speed train from London (Paddington) to Plymouth and back behind three of the Western's *Castles*. (Apart from the preserved *King*

George V, the Kings had by then all gone to their long rest.)

The special excursion was to commemmorate the 60th anniversary of the Ocean Mails Special, when *City of Truro* had reached a maximum of 102.4 mph between Plymouth and Bristol and the aim to beat that record and try to 'do the ton' on the last leg back from Bristol to London. The problem was to find engines fit enough to do the job, for by this time there was only one route regularly using express steam; those finally chosen were Nos 4079 *Pendennis Castle,* 5054 *Earl of Ducie* and the double-chimneyed 7029 *Clun Castle.* Their selection was both emotive and practical. No 4079 was the engine which was used in the GWR/LNER exchange trials of 1925 and which beat the latter company's Gresley Pacific's on its own ground; No 5054

was the free runner for the 100 mph trial and No 7029 was shown to be the best for the record attempt.

On the day there was both failure and success. Poor *Pendennis Castle* melted her fire bars and had to be taken off. Then there followed an almost unbelievable run behind No 6999 *Capel Dewi Hall,* which took the train on to Taunton with a maximum speed of 86½ mph – a great achievement for 6-ft coupled wheels – then a reserve (No 7025 *Sudeley Castle*) took the train to Plymouth. The journey home was, on the whole, a success, in that No 7029 *Clun Castle,* with 265 tons behind her tender, was at least four minutes up on *City of Truro* on her stretch with a maximum speed of 96 mph; *Earl of Dulcie* also recorded 96 mph. It was a great day and one when, to use the words of that great writer on steam,

New Zealand's Ja class 4-8-2s were handsome engines and they handled a great deal of traffic well into the late 1950s including the Gisborne–Wellington expresses in the North Island

The huge Kb 4-8-4s joined the Ja class in being New Zealand's most widely-used steam locomotives at home on both passenger and freight trains. This picture of a Kb on a Christchurch–Arthur's Pass freight was taken as recently as 1966

above
A particularly notorious and dramatic incline to be worked by steam was New Zealand's Rimutuka. It was a Fell centre rail installation with a grade of 1 in 15 and special steam tank engines, sometimes five to a train, thundered their way up the hill from Cross Creek

top
By the 1960s steam was becoming even more elusive in England and most branch lines, once worked by diminutive tank engines, had either become 'dieselised' or disappeared altogether. A typical example was the GWR branch from Berkley Road to Lydney which used 0-4-2 tanks built in the 1930s but with a basic design going back to Victorian times

the late Cecil J. Allen, to have mentioned the word diesel would have seemed like brawling in church.

By this time, more and more enthusiasts were roaming the world with their cameras. Some went to Finland to find wood-burning 2-8-0s near to the Arctic Circle, some to watch the end of French main-line steam behind Pacifics, Mountains and the 141R 2-8-2s from the New World, imported to fill a vital need at the end of the Second World War; others went to Germany, some to Eastern Europe and some to the great stronghold of elderly locomotives, Spain. Here one could find the venerable as well as the modern at work on gauges both broad and narrow. There were old American Baldwin 2-8-0s rubbing shoulders

with locomotives from the Swiss Rhaetian Railway, metre and stand-ard-gauge Garratts and Pacifics as well as varying forms of Mallets. For a decade it was a rail fan's paradise and, what is more, one where the enthusiast was welcomed.

This was not always the case further east but if one wanted to find regular steam in Europe in profusion in the late 1960s and early 1970s there was little option. It was in Eastern Europe in 1967 that the disciples of T.R. Perkins met up with those of Rogers Whitaker. These were the early days of enthusiast incursion into that area and it was both exciting and intriguing. The author once joined some friends on an excursion in that direction; our tour was provided with charming lady guides in both Czechoslovakia and Hungary. There

was less understanding than now of the slightly odd hobby and railway photography was not easy, although the guide, Margaret, did her best. When three of us wanted to go into Austria by rail instead of by boat up the Danube, as planned, persistence won the day and out by train we went, leaving poor Margaret to explain why her group exit visa was three short at the border. It was, incidentally, on that trip that the author first met the famous Rogers Whitaker.

By the 1970s Africa, where railway changes were only just beginning, had become a magnet for enthusiasts. Already East Africa had independence and there were signs of difficulties arising further south. In the 1930s it had been possible to take a boat to Lobito on the west coast of

above
The last main-line express train service to be worked by steam in Britain was that from London (Waterloo) to Bournemouth. These remained because of modern electrification works taking time for completion but came to an end in the summer of 1967. The locomotives were mostly Bulleid designed Pacifics in their rebuilt form

above, right
As steam retreated in Europe enthusiasts began to seek some of the countries where its early demise was imminent and where interesting locomotives were still at work, including Finland's wood-burning 2-8-0s

right
The Spanish 4-8-4s, their largest and most modern engines, still hauled the *La Coruna* express as late as 1968

Portuguese Angola and travel by
train over the British-owned Benguela railway to the Congo border,
then through Northern Rhodesia,
over Victoria Falls bridge, through
Southern Rhodesia to South Africa.
Now this journey is not possible for
passengers, although the tracks are
there and, in spite of political problems, freight trains still run. In 1973 it
seemed time to have a look at the
railways of Southern Africa once
again and to begin with Angola.

The Benguela Railway was the
most remote and enchanting of any
of the African lines and the trip over it
proved to be well up to expectations.
Its long single track probes deep into
African countryside; its engines are
mainly modern Beyer Garratts from
Manchester; its locomotive depots
are surrounded by eucalyptus forests
and most of the line's steam power
burns this indigenous fuel.

The journey begins at Lobito from
a station adjacent to the Terminus
Hotel, run by the railway and set on
the side of a silver sand shore. The first
stage, to the port of Benguela itself, is
along a semi-suburban line and on
this stretch the engine was a coal-

burning 11th class 4-8-2 built by the
North British Locomotive Company. The main train of the day was
the Mail, going all the way through
to the Congo border. Most of the
passengers join at Benguela, where
the engine was changed for an oil-
burning Garratt, a 4-8-2 + 2-8-4 built
as late as 1956. At the time of our visit
the new cut off which now avoids
some of the worst grades to Cubal
had not yet been opened but all other
trains as far as this first stop of
consequence were already diesel
hauled.

The train left Benguela around 6
pm and as it twisted round reverse
curves it was possible to look forward
and see the locomotive almost at
right angles to the rear of the train,
with the flare of the oil flames darting
into the darkness.

As the morning light filtered
through the blinds of the sleeping-
compartment window it was ac-
companied by an unfamiliar but
very pleasant smell – the train was
now being hauled by a very rare
species: a wood-burning Garratt. At
almost every crossing post there was
a freight making its way down to

One of the gems of the Portuguese standard gauge was this baby 0-4-0 tank used as shed pilot at Porto for many years

Eastern Europe also came up with its gems. This old Austrian-designed double-framed 0-6-0 was still at work in Hungary, lovingly cared for in 1974

The Benguela Railway in Angola, running from the Atlantic Coast at Lobito to the border of Zaire, uses mainly British built steam, much of it wood burning. When the line was in its prime all locomotives and stock were in superb order, repairs being carried out in the main shops at Nova Lisboa. Eastwards from there trains were hauled by modern North British built 4-8-2s, a wood-burning class

Benguela. Looking at the wagons one could see that they came from Zambia, Zaire and Katanga as well as great loads of coal from the Wankie mines in Rhodesia. It seemed a strange world where politics necessitated one line of action and economics another.

By mid-morning we were into Nova Lisboa, the hub of the system, which also contained the workshops where all repairs and rebuilding take place and where the works shunter was one of the old rack engines once used on a now abandoned section further west. Here our Garratt came off and was replaced by a sparkling 4-8-2 built by North British in 1951; she too was a wood-burner. We were

fortunate enough to have footplate permits and it was a completely new experience to watch eucalyptus logs being expertly thrown into the fire-box. There was a crew of three: driver, fireman and wood passer, the latter standing on the tender on top of a vast pile of logs and tossing them down two at a time.

East of Nova Lisboa the country-side flattens out and heavier trains are worked, it being the rule rather than the exception for a second Garratt to be cut into the middle of a long train. En route we made several stops at anonymous places to *log up,* the loco coming to rest alongside a huge mound of eucalyptus wood. Most of the Mail trains terminated at Silva

One of the unusual features of the Benguela Railway was its eucalyptus forests specially grown for the wood-burning engines. These were 'logged up' at their home depots and at several special stops during the course of their journey

Porto, since passenger traffic beyond there was thin and in any case at that time this was becoming terrorist country.

On the return trip we had the same 11th class North British 4-8-2 and the experience of riding back on this engine will never be forgotten. As darkness fell a huge plume of bright red but quickly-dying embers shot from the chimney, covering the whole train like a firework display but burning out before touching the ground. As one looked out there were the banks of eucalyptus trees carefully planted in groves on the side of the track. The fireman would throw in about twelve logs or so every three or four minutes and the scented smoke drifted back, partly from the firehole door and partly on the evening breeze.

Safari by rail certainly has its moments.

Minor Railways

Mixed Train Daily is the title of one of the most evocative books on the subject of little trains. It appeared in 1947, and there is little doubt that its publication was timely enough to spark off an interest the world over not only in the little trains of America but also wherever else they ran. The author was that famous American writer Lucius Beebe and his photographer Charles Clegg. The pair had toured the United States – sometimes in their ornate private saloon added to the rear of a bumbling local – seeking out the past while there was time; their stated aim was to record the old, the enfeebled, the venerable and the fragrant with legend.

The little trains of the world were once a vital part of local communications. Most were found in the countryside linking hamlets and villages with the district's market towns. Some, like the Rotterdam Steam Tram, still running in the early 1960s, linked the market towns with the big city. By that time the tramway was 'dieselised', steam being used for specials or in emergencies only

The Reseau Breton was one of France's finest narrow gauge systems. There were railcars for most passenger trains, 0-6-6-0 Mallet tanks for freight, and 4-6-0 tanks (seen here) for the odd *extra* or for special trains

Until the Second World War most of the world's enthusiasts were British or American and they were divided from each other by a wide stretch of water. Accordingly, each group was insular in outlook; then came the war, when enforced journeys across the Atlantic made many enthusiasts of both countries conscious of the world of railways outside their own homeland. Thus *Mixed Train Daily* not only woke up the American enthusiast to a realisation of a rapidly passing scene, it also roused a deep interest in Britain, where the country railway was soon also to be in grave danger of extinction. Lines built to serve rural Britain were in decline, although they had been saved for a while by wartime necessity.

Throughout the world the little trains had become part of the countryside; to the villages and hamlets they were the connection with the faster but distant world of the cities, as familiar as the postman and as re-assuring as the ringing of the church bells. Usually, the trains themselves were antique, for little money was available to renew or even repair; the tracks skirted hillsides, ran along river banks and through main streets of villages, perhaps towards a tiny terminus marked only on large-scale maps. It was the early 1950s before the enthusiast with his cameras really realised what was happening – and by then it was the eleventh hour.

Like so many aspects of the railway hobby, this interest in the rural line served several ends. For the more technically minded there was the almost unbelievable variety of locomotives and rolling stock, often cast-offs from the arrogant and powerful main lines and, on the narrow gauge, remnants of Victorian antiquity kept

going by local ingenuity. Above all, there was the charm of discovery, to travel into the unknown in Brittany or Colorado, the Hartz Mountains or the wilderness of Calabria, not to mention the delights of Western Ireland. Sometimes the trains conveyed passengers, more often only freight, although a passenger van on the rear was often used unofficially by local people. As soon as matters returned to 'normal', closures began in earnest and there was little time for action.

Among others, Beebe and Clegg recorded the American scene; they visited the classics, the East Tennessee and Western North Carolina Railroad, 'Tweetsie' for short, the Rio Grande Southern, the Owens Valley branch of the Southern Pacific and the route of the Denver & Rio Grande Western's (and America's) only narrow gauge named train, the

San Juan. They also looked at such byeways as the Aberdeen & Rockfish R.R. in North Carolina, the legendary Virginia & Truckee, the logging lines and the wood burners. And at an almost infinite variety of locomotives: Baldwins and Alcos, moguls and consolidations, Shays and other forms of geared locomotion; some were beautifully kept and maintained – the Virginia & Truckee still polished their chimney caps – and some just about kept going. Trains varied from the Denver & Rio Grande's *San Juan* to the once weekly freight over a remote section of the Rio Grande Southern. The countryside in which they ran ranged from the mountains of Colorado, the rolling hills of Virginia and the pasture lands of Vermont to the coal mines of industrial Pennsylvania.

Today there is very little left of these railroads, although some have

Another narrow-gauge network, of some size, in France radiated from Tulle in the Correze. This comprised two systems, the Correze Tramway and the narrow gauge lines of the old Paris–Orleans Railway. The last to remain was the PO line from Tulle to Argentat; the motive power was 0-4-4-0 Mallet tanks

been rescued by private enterprise as tourist operations. Two isolated sections of the once huge Denver & Rio Grande Western narrow gauge network still work regularly during the summer months, although this is in no way due to altruism on the part of that company. First there is the 45-mile line branching from Durango to the old mining town of Silverton, which lasted to run a twice weekly (Tuesday and Saturday) passenger service into the 1950s, the journey being scheduled to take some three hours but actually taking nearer five. Trains hauled by ageing 2-8-2s heaved their loads into the mountains along stone ledges just wide enough to accommodate the track, with curves so sharp that the engine ran at right angles to the rear vehicle. So popular did the run become with tourists that the Rio Grande had eventually to make this a daily train in summer, but with winter maintenance high and washouts a frequent occurrence, it was scarcely economic and closure was sought. A campaign was organised to combat abandonment and because of the line's unique interest, closure was forbidden by the authorities. Today

the train winds its way, twice daily during the summer months, through the canyons of the Animas River to the reconstructed town of Silverton, where the saloons have been re-opened and mock gunfights shatter the silence of the hills. The other section of the Denver & Rio Grande Western which is still worked is the 67-mile line from Chama (New Mexico) to Antonito (Colorado) described in Chapter 5.

In Europe the sun was also setting over the minor railways and country branch lines. The Second World War saw the end of some of the little trains; invading armies were no respecters of mini railways which got in their way, and afterwards there was no money and little inclination for restoration. In spite of this, a remarkable number lasted well into the 1960s, some into 1970s and a few still survive today. All kinds and conditions of steam motive power existed, from tram engines with metal skirts over their wheels, to powerful Mallet compound tanks. These ran the freights alongside the newer petrol and diesel passenger railcars until the car, the bus and the

above
These little *Terrier* tanks of the old
London Brighton & South Coast Railway
were used to work several of Britain's
Light Railways up to the Second World
War. They were light, economical and
simple. Several are now preserved and
running on tourist lines

opposite, above
The largest Irish narrow-gauge railway as
well as one of the last to operate was the
County Donegal Railways Joint Committee.
This was one of the border crossing lines
necessitating customs examinations with
consequent delays but its red and cream
railcars and geranium red 4-6-4 and 2-6-4
tanks were still working until the end of
1959

opposite, below
Austria is a mountainous country and a
natural home for narrow-gauge trains.
One of those to make full use of its
tourist potential is the Zillertal Railway
running out of Jenbach to Mayrhofen
using 0-6-2 tanks. Steam rarely runs
except during the summer months

lorry ultimately took over. Fortunately there was just time for European
enthusiasts and historians to cover
most of this vast field.

In Britain their demise had begun
during the depression of the 1930s,
and by 1939 most of the short
independent lines not swallowed up
by the grouping of the railways in
1923 had either closed or were in
serious trouble. Of those remaining,
the standard-gauge lines under the
control of the late Colonel Holman
Stephens still used ancient second-
hand engines for motive power.
Terrier tanks from the old London
Brighton & South Coast
railway – diminutive engines with
six-coupled wheels – still travelled
over the amusingly initialled Weston,
Cleveland & Portishead Railway in
Somerset as well as the Kent & East
Sussex Railway out of Tenterden
Town, but the Selsey Tramway had
gone and the Edge Hill Light Railway never began to operate. Wales
still had steam on most of its charming little narrow-gauge lines, built to
carry slate, a commodity for which
demand was dying, and the Great
Western Railway still ran the Welshpool & Llanfair section through the
fields of Powys.

The closure of the branch lines
began in earnest in the 1950s. In
England, Scotland and Wales ancient
tank engines and 0-6-0s had retreated
to these havens as if hard pressed by an
alien invader – as indeed they were,
for the muttering of the diesel engine
was becoming louder year by year. It
was mostly the country lines which
were swept away: the haunts of the
Great Western Dean Goods 0-6-0s,
some of which had seen service in
two World Wars; the homes of the
diminutive Stroudley *Terriers,* once
painted in the Brighton Company's
improved engine green – really a form of
yellow – and the sole remaining 2-4-
0s, the Great Eastern E4s, in East
Anglia. The market towns also lost
their train services as livestock and
other farm produce came in by road.
Such places as Tewkesbury, Wells,
Kington and Eardisley were all fore-
saken; so were the villagers of Llanfair Caereinion, who sent their cattle
and sheep to Welshpool market every
Monday on the special narrow-gauge
train hauled by *The Earl* or *Countess,*
little 0-6-0 tanks once owned by the
Cambrian Railways.

Over in Ireland, the many narrow-
gauge trains continued to run and
served the country districts well. To

left
In East Germany a 99 class 0-4-4-0 Meyer tank waits at Steinbach with a train from Wolkenstein to Johstadt

right
Once, and not so long ago, Spain had more steam-operated narrow-gauge lines than most countries in Europe. Now the only line of consequence is the lengthy coal carrying Ponferrada–Villablino railway. A pair of Engerth 2-6-0s take a Ponferrada-bound coal train through a gorge near Paramo

below, right
Running to the market town of Gmund on the Czech border, one of Austria's state-owned narrow-gauge lines uses an unusual form of semi-articulated engine, an Engerth, for its motive power

below
Portugal still uses narrow-gauge steam in some quantity although the frequent suburban services out of Porto Trindade station rarely see the modern Henschel 2-8-2 tanks now that diesels have arrived

many the Irish narrow gauge was the great attraction. Over the years of the nineteenth century and the early ones of the twentieth a network of these railways had been built with government aid to provide rural transport facilities and bring prosperity to remote areas. In the event, their trains more often carried emigrants eastwards and hastened depopulation of the very places which the lines were intended to stabilise. Some, such as the Londonderry & Lough Swilly, with its extension to the wild western coast of Donegal at Burtonport and the County Donegal Railways Joint Committee (owned by the Great Northern of Ireland and the Midland of England) were railways of considerable length and much traffic, others were really more glorified roadside tramways; all had 'character' in their own right. There were the West Clare Railway – made famous by Percy French with his song 'Are Ye Right There Michael, Are Ye Right?' and noted also for an anemometer at Quilty to measure the wind force lest trains be blown over in gales; the Cavan and Leitrim which served Ireland's only commercial source of coal; and the Tralee & Dingle, without question the most exciting of all the lines.

What a railway this Tralee & Dingle was! By the 1950s its 33 miles of 3 ft 0 in gauge line, Europe's most westerly, was one of the world's great pieces of adventurous railroading. Its only trains were cattle specials which ran on the last weekend of every month over track which could scarcely be seen for grass; it climbed precipitous gradients of 1 in 30 and its engines, ancient 2-6-0 Hunslet tanks, required the faculties of a Kerry goat. In short, as the local people put it, it was 'a grand railway'. The maximum permitted load was eighteen vehicles, made up of seventeen bogie cattle vans and one passenger brake van converted into part-cattle wagon, part-goods van. At least one such van had the handbrake in the middle of the cattle portion! On discovering this, the language of any non-regular Tralee & Dingle man shanghaied into the job had to be heard to be believed!

Apart from those lines serving the peat bogs, the last narrow-gauge railway to run in Ireland was the West Clare, which closed in 1960, by which time it was 'dieselised.' The last to use steam was the County Donegal, with a main line from Londonderry to Donegal, via Strabane, and branches to Letterkenny, Ballyshannon and Killybegs. This magnificent line used railcars for its passenger services from the mid-1920s and this economy helped to keep it alive. The freights were worked by geranium red 4-6-4 and 2-6-4 tank engines carrying such names as *Erne, Columbkille, Meenglas* and *Blanche*. Steam also worked the bank holiday specials to Ballyshannon, the last of which ran on August Bank Holiday Monday in 1959. On the return journey the second of the day's two specials was worked by *Blanche* and the memory of that run remains very clear. Beyond Barnesmore Halt the line began to climb at 1 in 60 for three miles into the mountains, over one of the most spectacular sections of any Irish railway. Clinging to the slopes high over road and river, the train appeared as a slow-moving model against the mountain landscape. *Blanche* was throwing out great clouds of smoke and this drifted down to the watchers who had come to see the last rites. Soon the road and rail came close together near the summit and cars drew up and hands waved as *Blanche* made her way along the high embankment, her train snaking behind, just as the sun dropped below the hills. It was a moving moment.

left
The Corgo line from Regua to Chaves is one of the several branching northwards from the standard-gauge Douro Valley branch of the Portuguese State Railway. What is more, it is still one hundred per cent steam and continues to use the unique 2-4-6-0 Mallet tanks

below
Further east along the Douro Valley is the narrow-gauge Tua line still using ancient outside cylinder 2-6-0 tanks for its freights and mixed trains

As in Ireland, so too in Europe, most of the minor railways were constructed to assist the economy of the more rural areas and were subsidised in one form or another by central or local government. At the height of this period of operation – one could scarcely call it 'prosperity' – it would have been possible, with comparatively few breaks, to have journeyed over their tracks from the North Sea to the Mediterranean. There were so many of these railways that it is only possible here to mention a few.

The French were among the leading exponents in the art of both the obvious and the hidden subsidy for railways – some small companies were even owned by the mighty SNCF, the national state railway organisation, but leased to operators who ran the little trains on its behalf. Perhaps the best example of this is the Reseau Breton – using the present tense because one arm of what was once a many-pointed star still operates – which is now converted to standard gauge. The network, radiating from Carhaix in Brittany, had a total of 267 miles of track and was the largest secondary railway in France. Its trains were worked by powerful 0-6-6-0 Mallet tanks, 4-6-0

tanks and numerous railcars. Even in its leanest times, as long as the system was complete (and it remained so until well into the 1960s) at least eleven steam trains and thirty-eight railcars arrived and departed every day on its five radiating lines. In more recent years steam worked the freights, plus the occasional *Mixte,* like the twice-weekly train from Camaret, in the far-distant west, to Chateaulin. This ran on Tuesday and Saturdays, being only *facultatif* for the rest of the week, depending upon the supplies of *langoustes* shipped alive from the little harbour in crates packed with ice and sent to all parts of France. The regular engine for such trains was No 332, a 4-6-0T of ancient lineage. It is still easy to picture the scene: the brownish smoke pouring from the engine's chimney, the cab floor littered with coal briquettes and a train of four or five wagons and a solitary coach; the whole forming the day's *marchandises-voyageurs.* The coach

was a composite, one part second class and the other third, the former being furnished with seats. Between the two sections was a small compartment containing an ancient wash basin which was once part of the lavatory accommodation – a facility not available in later years. Everything waited upon the arrival of the regular railcar, which would appear, on time, scattering chickens as it entered the station yard. The *Chef de Gare* raised his arm, No 322 sprayed adjacent onlookers with a mixture of water, steam and briquette smoke and departed. The clock stood at 9.45 am.

At Chateaulin the passengers who wished to venture further left to enter a railcar for Carhaix, the company's mechanical headquarters where, in the large shed and works, were the massive 0-6-6-0 Mallet tanks which hauled the regular freights to Guingamp, Morlaix, Rostrenen and Loudeac.

Austria still has a number of minor

above
Steam no longer operates over Portugal's southernmost narrow-gauge system based on Sernada da Vouga. Back in the 1960s this line used a variety of steam engines including 2-6-0 tanks, 2-4-6-0 Mallet tanks and 2-8-2 tanks

above, right
Italy has little steam in use today but, surprisingly, some of this is on the narrow gauge. The once vast Ferrovie Calabria–Lucane, in the South, makes use of 2-6-0 and 0-8-0 tanks for freight. These squat and rather ugly engines have been seen heading the occasional enthusiast special during recent years

right
One of the very few standard-gauge rack railways in the world is in Roumania. Its engines are rack and adhesion tanks pulling the train in the normal manner on the more level stretch out of Subletate, reversing to push it up and brake it down the steep climb and descent to Boutari. It is very much a country line and its future could be in doubt

44

lines, some of which, such as the Steyrtalbahn and the Zillertal, use steam regularly. The latter has its junction connection with the state railway – the mighty Osterreich Bundesbahn – at Jenbach, as does the delightful little Achenseebahn line, with its three rack and pinion 0-4-0 tanks, two of which date from 1888. One of several remarkable oddities about the Achenseebahn is that it is still there; a very good road has been built to its upper terminus but the little engines still work their slow and thunderous way up the rack section, doing their dignified best to disregard the fact that, due to the complications of rack motion the driving wheels appear to be revolving the wrong way!

On the other side of the OBB station at Jenbach is the Zillertalbahn (Silver Valley Railway), which is a less exciting but a busier line. Though diesels are now used on most trains the little Krauss 0-6-2 tanks still head summer passenger trains up the 1 in 40 gradient towards Mayrhofen, a delightful resort in the heart of the mountains.

Until a decade ago Spain was the hunting ground for European narrow-gauge steam enthusiasts, with such treasures as the brilliant green locomotives of the metre-gauge Economic Railways of Asturias, the Santander-Bilbao in the Cantabrian hills, the La Robla and the Alcoy-Gandia, with its lovely 2-6-2 Beyer-Peacock tanks dating from 1890. Today there is little of consequence left, except for the Ponferrada-Villablino line, which is now the only completely steam worked narrow-gauge public railway in Spain.

This railway was built to provide an outlet for the coal mines in the Villablino area and a considerable quantity of coal is still carried on the line. There are also two passenger trains each way daily, taking just over two hours for the 62 km journey. The locomotives used show the sales power and quality of both the American and German manufacturers: most were built by Baldwin, Krauss, Boris or Maffei.

Portugal, too, was a steam Mecca of great repute. Sadly it has also suffered a decline in the number of its narrow-gauge steam engines. Once there were three main groups of metre-gauge tracks in the north of the country; one was based on Porto, where an excellent suburban service was powered by 2-6-0 tanks, 2-8-2 tanks and the 0-4-4-0 Mallet tanks, with gleaming copper-capped chimneys. Today the service is mainly provided by diesel power.

Moving eastwards, there are still four picturesque lines, each separate, running northwards from the

above
Swiss narrow gauge steam still lingers on in preserved form on several mountain railways, although one, the Rothornbahn running out of Brienz on the shores of that lake still uses steam regularly. Diesels were beginning to take over in 1977

right
Some of the most dramatic of all Europe's narrow-gauge railways were built by the Austrians in what is now Yugoslavia. The longest by far ran from Belgrade to Dubrovnik on the Adriatic coast via Sarajevo – a journey taking the better part of two days. In later days the engines were 0-8-2s with large spark-arresting chimneys, and 2-8-2s

Douro Valley: the Tamega, Corgo, Tua and Sabor lines, two of which use the unusual 2-4-6-0 Mallet tanks. There was also a system, now working entirely with diesel, based on Sernada da Vouga. This had a Borsig 4-6-0 and Henschel 2-8-2 tanks in addition to the classes mentioned earlier. The memorable thing about the Portuguese steam locomotives was their cleanliness – unfortunately, something of the past.

These narrow-gauge railways of Portugal are now a delightful anachronism but as a result of recent legislation their lives may yet be prolonged, mainly by the use of railcars for passenger services. The railways run, as do most other narrow-gauge lines, where economy is limited and depend upon only a few natural resources. Most link the towns and villages along river banks and take the seeker of genuinely rural life into terrain which is also full of history. This is an added attraction to the wide variety of tank engines which are in use; together they make this lovely land a 'must' for those who want to see a little of yesterday while there is still the time to do so. Today there is no broad gauge steam in Portugal but, at the time of writing, 2-4-6-0 tanks

are still used exclusively on the Corgo line to Chaves. Three steam trains run daily on the Tua line and 0-4-4-0 Mallets work on the Miranda branch.

One other western European country still runs narrow-gauge steam on occasions – Italy. Although the little line which served the Val Gardena in the Dolomites has long since gone, down in the south there is the 95 cm gauge Ferrovie Calabria-Lucane system. This comprises a group of geographically isolated lines spread over the heel and toe of Italy. It's most easterly point is Bari, on the Adriatic. Passenger services are worked by railcar but the freight trains are steam, headed by squat, ugly-looking 2-6-0 and 0-8-0 tanks. One particularly interesting feature is a rack section between Catanzaro Lido and Catanzaro Citta where 2-6-2 rack and adhesion tanks are used, usually on Sundays, when traffic is too heavy for the railcars. Strangely enough, the FCL makes contact with one of Europe's two standard-gauge rack lines which are open to passenger traffic (this is from Cosenza to Paola on the Mediterranean coast; the other is in Roumania). There are still some steam-operated narrow-gauge workings in Sicily but these

only carry freight. Like the FCL system the portents are that these will not be long for this world.

Most travellers and tourists see their mountain railways in Switzerland. The Swiss steam trains are of quite a different character, kept, as are so many things in that country, for the benefit of the tourist with money to spend. In particular the steam-operated Brienz-Rothorn rack railway just outside Interlaken is well worth a visit; some diesels are already in service here and, once again, time is running out. Swiss railways are usually clinically clean and efficient and several occasionally bring out the odd steamer to coax extra francs out of the pockets of both the package tourist and the discriminating rail fan.

Whilst T. R. Perkins pursued his difficult and intriguing task of travelling over Britain's railways and Rogers Whitaker is still aiming at *three million* miles of rail travel, your author has tended to love the railway bye-ways and to visit those that have been available within the compass of his attainments. Of these some of the most dramatic were in Yugoslavia, originally of Austrian construction and built prior to the First World War, when this area was part of the

Austro-Hungarian Empire. The narrow gauge in Yugoslavia is, or rather was, in the main the result of the Austrian possession of Bosnia, Herzegovina and Dalmatia; the railways were built principally to improve military communications.

Large areas of Yugoslavia are bare and rocky, with a number of mountain ranges to be crossed by railways which are consequently heavily graded: in past years narrow-gauge lines proved the rule rather than the exception. Multitudinous U-tunnels bored through rock faces and stone walls buttressing the tracks against precipitous cliffs as the lines climbed higher and higher into the hills, with the scenery becoming wilder and bleaker and the curves more tortuous. Today most of these lines are closed, with traffic diverted to newly-built standard-gauge railways but some, for example those from Visegrad to Sarajevo and from Mostar to Dubrovnik, are still there. Steam, once ubiquitous, is now almost superseded by American-built diesels and railcars. For years the main motive power consisted of powerful adhesion engines and one class of rack locomotive. Normal motive power included 73 class Krauss 2-6-2s of 1907 and later the

efficient and popular 83 class 0-8-2s and 85 class 2-8-2s built by Krauss, Jung at Budapest and, after the Second World War at Slavonski Brod. Once there was even a class of 2-6-6-0 Mallet tanks to bank 2-6-6-0 Mallets hauling heavy freights over the high mountains from Visegrad eastwards through the spiralling tunnels.

Depending upon the definition of a 'narrow-gauge' railway line the African continent is either almost solidly narrow gauge – for most of its trackage is either 3 ft 6 in or metre gauge – or there is comparatively little. Assuming, however, that the term is defined as 'less than the customary gauge', then there is a relatively small percentage. Even main-line trains in Africa are by their nature slow and usually the main form of transport for the indigenous population to whom time is not too important. Branch or narrow gauge trains are even slower.

Egypt once had a flourishing narrow-gauge system in the Nile delta area, these lines were in effect local tramways feeding the Egyptian State Railway's main line between Cairo and Alexandria.

In Equatorial Africa could and can be found some magnificent speci-

Mozambique has a delightful museum-piece line based on Jao Belo on the banks of the Limpopo River. It uses American built engines – Alco 2-6-os and a unique Baldwin 2-8-o woodburner with a huge cab

mens from time to time – the main problem is to get at them. An example of this is the fascinating 2 ft o in gauge line in Angola, running from Canocha on the CFM through the hills and forests to remote coffee plantations, with trains hauled by little wood-burning tank engines. To see the crowds waiting at the junction station for the twice daily mixed was to see Africa in full colour – the steaming forested hills in their varying hues of green, the native village with its traditional huts and the population clad in all the colours of the rainbow.

South Africa still keeps most of its narrow-gauge systems and these have been mentioned elsewhere in this book. On the Port Elizabeth to Avontuur line 'dieselisation' has already begun but elsewhere the well-maintained baby Garratts, built over the years by Beyer Peacock, Hanomag and Hunslet-Taylor, do their job well. Each carries its brightly-polished numberplate, sometimes with coloured backgrounds to the letters; the approxi-

mate age of these locomotives can easily be told by a look at these plates – the older generation carry the words South African Railways at the top of the plate and the Afrikaans equivalent on the bottom. On later plates this situation is reversed.

Further north, well inside one-time Portuguese territory is yet another piece of Africa's narrow gauge. Sadly, Mozambique is no longer open to the rail fan but it contains one of Africa's gems – a superb museum piece based on Joa Belo alongside the banks of the Limpopo river and some 200 km from Laurenco Marques. The engines are American – Alco 2-6-os and a Baldwin 2-8-o wood-burner. The latter, No o6, when last seen, was particularly well kept, with gleaming copper pipes, a silver-painted smokebox and three domes on the boiler, the whole almost dwarfed by a huge cab. What is more this line ran passenger trains – and probably still does. Where better to leave this charming, time avoiding and nostalgic subject of the little trains.

Steam today

It is difficult to be dogmatic as to exactly where the world's finest steam locomotives can be found today. Some enthusiasts like South Africa, with such delights as pairs of huge 4-8-4s double heading freight trains by the score out of Kimberley towards De Aar; others prefer the almost unbelievable variety of Indian locomotives still in action or perhaps modern Chinese *People* class Pacifics en route from Peking to Tientsin. To the author there is no doubt at all – the stars of the collection are in the Spice Islands of Indonesia. For sheer variety amongst exotic surroundings it is difficult to beat; it is not a place for steam-hauled main-line trains at speed but for ancients ambling out their lives it is unbeatable. The rostered power can range from nonagenarian British-built 2-4-0s to recent German and Japanese 0-10-0 rack tanks.

The Javanese are friendly people who welcome those interested in their railways but one must not expect the expected – it rarely happens – and train diagrams found in shedmasters' offices are often more decorative than informative. This lack of positive information, plus the steamy heat and occasional snakes can be a drawback. The majority of steam stock has been lying about for many years awaiting repairs and only a small proportion is usable at any one time. Nevertheless, with patience and perseverance the visitor can see a great deal, including such rarities as 0-4-0s, 2-4-0s, 4-4-0s and Mallets as well as more usual types. There is an almost infinite variety of tank engines from 2-12-2s

The exotic islands of Indonesia contain equally exotic steam engines. These include such rarities as 0-4-0 tender engines, ancient 2-4-0 centenarians and the huge Mallets which work out of Cibatu

to skirted 0-4-2s. The Surabaya steam tram system is particularly remarkable. This living piece of history still makes four regular trips a day using a wood-burning 0-4-0 tram locomotive painted blue, hauling two trailers with wooden seats and an occasional van. To see it screeching its way through the crowded streets of stalls, pedlars, discarded furniture, bicycles and people is to discover something truly of the old world; it is certainly a unique example. At the time of writing two tram engines are still in use, one British, one Dutch. How long they will last is anyone's guess but to see them all is well worth the price of an air ticket.

One problem is mobility – the various types and classes of locomotive are widely spread and almost impossible to see at work in a reasonable time by means of rail travel. On the other hand it is better not to drive yourself as you cannot then shut your eyes on appropriate occasions! It is also advisable to pick one's eating and sleeping places carefully! The interesting railways are not found adjacent to the luxury hotels of Bali, but rather in the kind

of places where by tradition the country folk prefer fingers to cutlery and the cleanliness of the fingers depends upon their owners.

In Java, apart from the Surabaya tram there are the active Mallets which climb out of Cibatu to Garabut with a mini train of two or three vans and a couple of dilapidated coaches. Maduin is the place for the vintage 2-4-0s and 4-4-0s and Cepu for some of the cleanest engines one can see in the world of steam today. Java also keeps a steam tourist railway; this, like most of the minor lines, runs when required and at Amberarwa this means when chartered. Amberarwa is in an idyllic setting with a back drop of mountains and a not inconsiderable lake. The line is part of a cross-country route, now closed to normal traffic and it is rack operated. The engines used are B 25 class wood-burning 0-4-2 rack and adhesion tanks which push a couple of coaches up the hill to Dedono and back, although at times it runs in the opposite direction along the edge of the water to Tuntango. The answer to an enquiry as to why it was not running was that it was for lack of wood – but that a

special could be run for half the price of the rack train! Times in the East do not change.

Over in Sumatra there is equal interest but an even greater need for mobility and patience, for it is a large island and the two main systems in the west and north are completely isolated by mountains and jungles. In the west a few 2-6-2 tanks work out of Padang but the main focus of interest is the rack tank working in both directions out of Padang Panjang. Some half a dozen of the 0-10-0 rack and adhesion engines are serviceable, including one of the older class D 18s (the modern engines are all fitted with Giesel ejectors). Coal is the real reason for the line's existence. This is worked from the mine to Solok by 2-12-2 tanks, which also take passenger trains and then by diminuitive 2-6-0 tanks, real veterans which make a fine sight hauling trains of modern steel bogie wagons to Batutebul where the rack loco takes over for the real climb to Padang Panjang. In the north of Sumatra some interesting wood-burning 2-4-2 tanks and 2-6-4 tanks on passenger and mixed trains can be found.

left
Another Javanese rarity is the Surabaya
steam tram – still in use today. The
engines are Dutch and British built 0-4-0
wood-burners

right
Sumatra has three separate railway
systems completely separated by
mountain barriers. One of these on the
west of the island is based on Padang
Panjang. This runs to the coal mines
beyond Solok and uses ten coupled rack
tanks, 2-6-0 tanks and 2-12-2 tanks. The
2-6-0 tanks make hard work of the coal
trains out of Solok

below
East Germany still uses steam in profusion
and much of it is still kept extremely
clean by today's standards, as shown by
this 2-6-2 leaving Dresden Neustadt with
a passenger train

So Java and Sumatra are musts for devotees. With the coming of diesels and the existence of oilfields the steam situation cannot last much longer.

North America and Australasia led the world in the race to eliminate steam traction and very little exists in these vast areas for the enthusiast seeking the Stephensonian heritage in regular service. Elsewhere steam traction is further entrenched, although in Europe it is under a Damoclean sword and time is running out fast.

There *is* still regular steam plying its smokey way in Europe but, with the recent demise of this in West Germany most operations are behind the Iron Curtain, where Perkins-type travel may be welcomed but cameras are often not. East Germany and Poland, both with ample supplies of coal, still maintain large fleets of steam locomotives to haul trains of all types, and what is more, the external and mechanical condition warrants more than a second glance – as indeed do the remnants of Czech steam. In recent years the Hamburg-Berlin expresses were hauled throughout by East German Pacifics – readily

photographable in West Germany, and a fine sight they were. Similarly the magnificent Czech 4-8-2s in blue livery which plied between Prague and Pilsen were worth the journey to see, even to take the risk of a not always warm welcome when taking photographs. What could have been better than the delights of old Prague, heady Pilsner beer and a blue 4-8-2 to boot?

Other countries/systems of Eastern Europe still run steam – some in profusion. Hungary in particular, has a few years to go before the orderly withdrawal of its magnificently kept shining black steamers in favour of diesels and electrics. After looking at the wonders of Buda, Pest and the Danube (with its genuine steam ships) a visit to the west station still finds huge shining 4-8-0s at work on long push and pull trains – a job more often carried out elsewhere in the world by tanks – whilst in the yards an ancient Austrian-designed 0-6-0 tank with double frames shunts the stock. Out in the flat plains round Lake Balaton and into the rolling hills more standard types are hard at work – particularly the 2-6-2s, 2-6-2 tanks, 2-4-2 tanks and sometimes, if

one is very lucky, a very elderly Austrian double-framed 0-6-0.

Yugoslavia has some steam, even some ex-United Nations Relief and Works Agency engines still at work both in their original British or American form, or 0-6-0 tanks on the American pattern but of indigenous construction. Pacifics, 4-8-0s, 2-6-2s and tanks still work the slower trains but the end is near – the ever encroaching American diesel industry has seen to that.

Bulgaria has steam, although mostly on freight trains. As with virtually all the European countries using this form of power, one of the ubiquitous machines is the ex-German – 2-10-0 Kriegslok – a wartime austerity engine which was built in huge numbers and has proved extremely successful. Bulgarian engines are painted green, with red frames and golden wings on the smokebox, a welcome change from the normal all embracing black. At Vakarel there is a large graveyard of withdrawn types, including some of the huge 2-12-4Ts and another elephantine creature, the 15M class 4-10-0. There is also some steam on the narrow gauge in the north of the country.

above
Until very recently the magnificent
Czech 4-8-2s in blue livery plied between
Prague and Pilsen hauling the inter-city
expresses. They were amongst the most
modern and efficient machines in Europe

left
Poland is another steamy country again
using Pacifics and other large motive
power on its expresses. Both East
Germany and Poland contain ample
reserves of coal and thus are able to make
continued economic use of steam power

right
Bulgaria uses some steam on her
standard-gauge tracks. Plovdiv is the
home of a number of these machines,
painted green with red frames and golden
wings on the smokebox doors

above
There is still one narrow-gauge system
using steam in Bulgaria, from Cervenbreg
to Orjahavo using green-painted 2-10-2
tanks

opposite
There is still a great deal of steam in
Turkey mainly on secondary work and
freight. One of the classics in use is the
German *Kriegslok* 2-10-0 which can be
found on many of the lines in the more
westerly areas including those out of
Izmir

left
There are some years to run before the
orderly withdrawal of Hungarian steam
locomotives is completed. One interesting
turn is the working of the large 4-8-0s on
push and pull trains out of Budapest West
station

Asia, perhaps, gives the modern rail fan his best reward, although, as in Eastern Europe, care is needed with photography. Turkey, part European but mostly Asian, is still steaming. Very little exists in European Turkey but east of the Bosphorus the situation changes for the better, and what is more the Turks are a very friendly people. Good centres include Izmir, Irmak (east of Ankara), Karabuk and Zonguldak and points east, including Sivas, Kars, Adana and Afyon. Whilst American influence predominates in the new diesel locomotives this is far from the case with steam power: here British and other European manufacturers have had their field days—mostly German, including omnipresent Kriegslok, showing not only the original Bismarkian policy of Drang Nach Osten but of political activity between the wars and during the Second World War. During the latter the British provided aid to Persia, Turkey, Iraq, Egypt and Palestine in the form of Stanier-designed LMS class 8F 2-8-0s; some of them are still at work in Iraq and Turkey. Although large engines to

British eyes, they are, of course, small for Turkish loads and are, these days, only used as yard shunters.

The largest fleet of steam locomotives remaining in the world today—and this by a substantial margin—is that of the Republic of India. Of those in the easily accessible world—that is, in countries where tourists can travel at will—it is the largest by a factor of at least five and, moreover, offers the greatest quality as well as quantity in its steam interest.

Steam haulage in India extends from prestige trains such as the *Taj Express* and *Darjeeling Mail* to humble freight and passenger locals on all three main gauges—5 ft 6 in, metre and 2 ft 6 in. With India having plenty of coal and until recently only a little oil, the policy of maintaining steam whilst developing diesel and electric traction is a sensible one. Including industrial steam locomotives, the total number in use is approximately 10,000.

Indian locomotive development in the days of British rule was based on two groups of standard designs. There were the British Engineering

During the Second World War Britain supplied a large number of LMS Stanier designed 2-8-0s for service in the Middle East; Turkey also obtained a few of these engines, some of which are still at work at Irmak near Ankara

Standards Association (BESA) locomotives of the early years of this
century and, between the wars, those
known as the Indian Railway Standards. Each group provided a range of
power for all duties on both the
metre and broad-gauge systems and
were used across the board on the
lines belonging to most of the companies which were then separate
entities. Each was typical of British
practice of the day and many examples survive in India, Pakistan, Sri
Lanka, Burma and Bangladesh. To
see a broad-gauge 4-6-0 at speed
through the Indian countryside in
the 1970s is to be transported back in
time.

Superimposed on the BESA and
IRS designs and now dominating the
workings is a further set of standard
locomotives of American inspiration, stemming from the WP 4-6-2
ordered from Baldwins of Philadelphia just before Indian Independence. A similar freight design,
the WG ('G' standing for Goods) 2-
8-2 has also been produced in large
numbers and there is a smaller 4-6-2
WL ('L' for Light) design too. The
appearance of these locomotives,

with their broad-gauge proportions,
is quite distinctive but the corresponding metre types have more
familiar lines. The handsome YP
4-6-2, the YG 2-8-2 (produced until
the early 1970s) and the YL 2-6-2 are
the corresponding and equally ubiquitous metre-gauge versions of the
broad gauge post Second World
War standard locomotives. The
majority were built in India, either at
the national locomotive works at
Chittajaran or by the private Telco
company.

On the 2 ft 6 in gauge the standard
IRS ZB 2-6-2, based on a Bagnell
design, has continued to be built for
India in many countries and used for
general purpose work on the extensive networks of this gauge.
Heavier ZE 2-8-2s can be found as
well and a few passenger 4-6-2s (the
ZPs) also exist but the type was not
perpetuated. The requirements of
the 2 ft 0 in gauge lines are rather
specialist and on the whole all the
narrow-gauge lines have tended to
keep their power from the days
before Independence for India meant
the end of independence for the
narrow-gauge railways.

The Germans supplied a large variety of
motive power to the Turks including
4-6-4 tanks for suburban services out of
Istanbul. One of these has now gravitated
to the Izmir area working a branch train
out of Manisa resplendent in green
livery – unusual for Turkey

The largest fleet of steam locomotives remaining in the world today is in the Republic of India. These include some fine semi-streamlined WP class Pacifics used to head such trains as the Malabar Express

Although locomotive design and allocation is the province of the central railway administration in Delhi, the various regional railways of India (Northern, Western, Central, Southern, South Eastern, Eastern, North Eastern and North-East Frontier) have their own locomotive fleets painted in their own liveries and this adds to the variety, especially in the large areas of the country where only locomotives of the standard ranges can be seen.

In most places, however, particularly as the gauge gets narrower, a plethora of non-standard power can be found, but on a highly localised basis. For example, the Darjeeling-Himalayan 0-4-0Ts, the most famous of all Indian locomotives, can only be seen on one little line in a corner of the country; this applies to much non-standard Indian steam and in fact an enthusiast who wants to see a high proportion of the types which are presently running needs months rather than weeks (as well as a strong constitution) to complete his collection over the vast sub-continent with its 36,000 miles of railway.

Although the diesel locomotive is in quantity production in India, many whole areas of the country remain 100 per cent steam and, hence, not only are a living reminder of what a busy steam railway was like but also are in many ways more British than BR. Certainly Indian Railways 1.7 million staff seem to contain a very high proportion of Anglophiles; and, indeed, English is the railways' official language, and the officials themselves still having their English titles. Any problems of travelling in India arise from the vast crowds and the (by European standards) unhygenic conditions rather than any lack of goodwill.

To the north is Nepal, the Kingdom of the Gods, tucked away between India's northern frontier and Tibet. There are tales of a fascinating 2 ft 6 in gauge system which forms the only means of transport for the locals and for the pilgrims at festival times. The fact that it ran over the border appears to be no hindrance to visitors who are supposed to enter Nepal via Katmandu. Engines include 4-6-0, 2-6-0 and 0-6-2 tanks, plus two 2-6-2 + 2-

6-2 Garratts named *Mahabir* (Monkey God) and *Sitarama* (King and Queen of the Gods). An interesting story is told of the first of the Garratts: Beyer Peacock sent an engineer out with the locomotive to take care of its introduction to service; the Nepalese were so pleased with the engine after it had been running for a few weeks that they paid the man, then and there, in gold bars!

The other gem is to the south of India – Sri Lanka, where steam lives on, but only just. Main line locomotives shunt the docks at Colombo, the capital, and they include the occasional B1 class 4-6-0 engines still carrying the names of one-time British governors. It is said that one of the two workable Garratt 2-6-2 + 2-6-2s sometimes emerges, albeit in terrible condition, from Nawalapitya shed. The last stronghold, if it can be called that, was Kandy, where morning and evening locals to Matale used B1 4-6-0s and B3 class No 22, a tender/tank locomotive of ancient times.

Much truncated but still in steam is the 2 ft 6 in gauge Kelani Valley line, which once ran from Colombo Fort to Openake: this is now open for just 15 miles or so. Some of the suburban workings are by Krupp diesels but the freights and mixeds still use Hunslet 4-6-4 tanks, some oil-burning and some coal.

Indian railwaymen take considerable pleasure in decorating their steeds and maintaining pride in the job, as with this YL class 2-6-2 on the Western Railway

right
Sri Lanka has one steam-operated narrow-gauge system based on Columbo – the Kelani Valley line. This is now somewhat truncated and only operates as a glorified suburban service using Hunslet 4-6-4 tanks and some diesels

below
To the south of India is Sri Lanka where steam lingers on – just. In its later years Kandy was a centre using 4-6-0s of British lineage

Most of the railways of South America were constructed with foreign capital, largely British and North American, and at the close of the Second World War many systems, notably in Argentina, still had very close connections with these countries. Despite nationalisation, operating practices, signalling, and so on still reflect the origins of these systems, now largely 'dieselised' but often with a scattering of steam power for shunting and local trip working.

Brazil has very little steam still active on the National system, a notable exception being the 75 cm gauge remnant of a once much more extensive system, now metre gauged. At São João del Rei, in the Belo Horizonte region, all freight and passenger trains are steam hauled over a system of some 200 km by a fleet of well maintained 2-8-0s, 4-6-0s and 4-4-0s, all supplied by North American builders between 1889 and 1912. In the south towards Porto Alegre the Dona Cristina coal railway (also now part of the National system) has become famous with enthusiasts, operating 2-6-6-2 Mallets, 2-10-4s and 2-8-2s of American origin. But beware, here diesels are impending! The sugar cane region around Campos and Recife have

below
One of India's most attractive lines is the Darjeeling–Himalaya Railway climbing up towards the roof of the world. Like many local lines it was built to serve a country community and acts as such by running through the streets

some amazing old locomotives, often ex main line, still in seasonal use, but here again the 'usinas' are turning more and more to road transport.

In Uruguay, a few standard gauge 4-6-0s and 2-6-0s of British origin linger on, while Argentina has pockets of steam operation on the metre gauge around Tucuman, on the standard gauge Urquiza system and on the broad gauge south of Buenos Aires at depots such as Tandil and Olavarria. In Buenos Aires there is a metre gauge steam at Tapailes; until recently there were passenger workings to La Plata. In the south, spectacular steam is to be found on the long 75 cm Esquel branch, and further south still on the Rio Turbio coal line. From Esquel a pleasant trip through snow capped mountains and the lake district leads to southern Chile, where plenty of rather run-down steam can be found; these are mostly 2-6-0s and 4-6-0s on passenger workings, and 2-8-2s and 4-8-2s on freight.

Paraguay is the only South American country to remain 100 per cent faithful to steam, and its British built fleet of 2-6-0s and 4-6-0s, all of which are wood burners, has changed little since the standard gauge railway was constructed to link Asuncion with the Argentine

above
Brazil has very little steam on its National system, but there is the 75 cm line at São João del Rei where a fleet of Baldwins are almost dazzling. In the foreground is a 4-6-0

left
Argentina uses a variety of British and American built steam and prior to nationalisation the British in particular had large stakes in the railway industry. Vulcan Foundry 2-8-0 No 4183 shunts the yard at Tandil, south of Buenos Aires

system via an ancient train ferry at Puerto Encarnacion.

Moving northwards little active steam is to be found in Peru with the notable exception of the 3 ft gauge Huancayo–Huancavalica line; this is reached over the famed 'highest and hardest' Central of Peru railway, one of the last in South America to be nationalised.

A few years ago Bolivia offered some active steam, including a few Garratts and 2-10-2s but steam has recently become very scarce here. Ecuador, with its famous 'devils nose' switchback climb between the coast and the capital, Quito, still has American-style railroading behind 2-6-0s and 2-8-0s on the coastal and mountain sections, and the Cuenca branch, although the rest of the country, including the capital, is now 'dieselised.'

Colombia, once the home of various types of articulated locomotives, now has very little steam, mostly in reserve, while railways have virtually been eliminated from Venezuela and Guyana.

Southern Africa remains for the time being, a Mecca, although political considerations and developments have placed a severe rein on the globe-trotting camera-toting enthusiast over the past few years and have certainly put a stop to Cecil

Rhodes' dream of a Cape to Cairo railway route. Because of one-time colonial interests, British designs somewhat naturally predominate in the southern African world of steam but in South Africa itself the German manufacturers, notably Henschels, have supplied many locomotives whilst in once Portuguese territory some American influences are noticeable.

South Africa maintains a large but dwindling fleet of well-kept steam locomotives, although the classes that work the retreating steam services are now largely standardised. The SAR is predominately a freight railway. Many lines have no official passenger service at all and others only mixed trains, while even main lines may only see a couple of passenger trains per day. The great Blue Train itself is now never hauled by a steam engine, although part of the route from Kimberly to De Aar, is one of the most famous steam lines in the world! This double track main line carries really heavy traffic, nearly all hauled by the huge 25NC class 4-8-4s. A visit to either Beaconsfield shed at Kimberley or to De Aar shed is a journey into the past with engines kept clean, smart and polished and there in numbers which the modern day enthusiast finds difficult to believe.

Two main lines for steam are those from Worcester, a few hours journey from Capetown, to Mosselbay, Oudtshoorn and Kliplaat en route to Port Elizabeth and that from Graaff Reinet to Rosmead. The first route carries the Capetown to Port Elizabeth, Garden Route express and the latter the Mosselbay—Johannesburg express. The Port Elizabeth train climbs over the fantastic Montague Pass whilst the Johannesburg train not only does this but takes in the Lootsberg pass as well. Today both trains are headed by class GEA 4-8-2 + 2-8-4 Garratts, although the latter uses a spotless and sparkling 19D class 4-8-2 from Oudtshoorn to Kliplaat. To see the huge Garratt articulated locomotives heaving their trains up the serpentine curves of the two mountain passes is one of the railway sights of the 1970s, even if they are run chimney trailing.

The one-time world famous route for SAR steam was that from Bloemfontein to Kronstad which once had steam trains every 10 minutes, but steam, at the time of writing, still worked the Orange Express from Bloemfontein to Kimberley.

Other centres of SAR steam include Burgersdorp, where the aging 15AR class 4-8-2s still work passenger trains to Aliwal North, and the East London and Port Elizabeth suburban services. Steam still reigns supreme on many branch lines but today the old classes are gone and standardisation is there in the form of 19D 4-8-2s and 24 class 2-8-4s.

One of the most interesting aspects of SAR steam is the number of narrow gauge 2 ft 0 in gauge lines which are still in full operation, including the long stretch of railway from Port Elizabeth to Avontuur. This now only uses steam from Assegaaibos to Avontuur, but it is still the thick end of a day's journey: the locomotives used are NG15 class 2-8-2s. The other narrow gauge sections are entirely in the hands of the delightful 'baby' Garratts – 2-6-2 + 2-6-2 engines, the last of which were built as late as 1968. The two busiest lines are south of Durban, running from Port Shepstone to Harding and from Umzinto to Donnybrook. There are also two 'one engine in steam' branches. The first runs from Umlaas Road to Mid Illovo but one of the most distinctive is that from Estcourt to Weenan – it

Paraguay, off the tourist's beaten track, still uses nothing but steam out of its colonial style station at Ascuncion. Still running are 4-6-0s, 2-6-2Ts and 2-6-0s. The works are at Sapucay, some 60 miles out of the capital. The 4-6-0s are ex-Argentina locomotives and the 2-6-0s seen below are North British Locomotive Company of 1910

South Africa is the home of big steam on the 3 ft 6 in gauge. Huge 4-8-4s still work main-line expresses over part of the system and the route from Kimberley to De Aar is one of the most famous steam lines in the world. Here, on that route, at Orange River all trains stop to take water and have their fires cleaned

has a blue engine! This is NG59, loved and cared for by its driver Billy Bester who makes all enthusiasts welcome.

South Africa also boasts some magnificent industrial steam, a very high percentage of which are ex-main line locomotives of types no longer used by SAR or Rhodesia. One can see red Garratts on heavy coal trains, blue 4-8-2s on empties and green 4-8-2Ts shunting.

Rhodesia and Zambia still use steam. although the latter country has turned over almost completely to diesel haulage. The great coal mine at Wankie in Rhodesia ensures continuing use of steam in that country, certainly for the time being. The central works are in Bulawayo and most steam operations are from there to Gwelo and northwards to Thompson Junction (for Wankie) and Victoria Falls. Even in recent politically trying times interchange traffic has been regularly taking place over the border of the two adjacent countries via the Victoria Falls bridge, each side backing its trains over the central border line and the other taking it away, the Rhodesians using their massive 20th class 4-8-2 + 2-8-4 Garratts. The Wankie Collieries have four unsuperheated 19th class 4-8-2s

plus three 16 DA light Pacifics imported from South Africa. All are housed in a cramped shed near the main shaft of No 2 colliery. Access is forbidden but the engines work the heavy coal trains to Thompson Junction over 1 in 80 gradients and here photography is easy. These engines are painted standard *Wankie Green* and are kept spotless. The Pacifics were used in earlier days in South Africa to work the *United Limited* express.

Some excellent steam working can still be found in East Africa, although with the break up of co-operation between Uganda, Kenya and Tanzania the once efficient and well-run East African Railways system is now fragmented. Nevertheless a visit to Nairobi is still very worthwhile and a friendly reception awaits those who seek permission to inspect the world's largest working steam engines, the huge red 59 class 4-8-2 + 2-8-4 Garratts and the smaller but equally efficient 60 class engines of similar wheel arrangement. The long distance overnight passenger trains to Mombasa with their restaurant and sleeping cars are diesel worked now but the frequent freights over the same route are still the domain of the huge Garratts. The climb up to Nairobi from Athi

above
One of the commonest African
locomotive types is the Garratt – used in
most countries in southern Africa. These
are still hard at work over the 'Garden
Route' from Worcester to Oudtshoorn
and from Kliplaat over the Lootsberg
Pass to Rosmead, hauling both passengers
and freight

left
One of South Africa's longer stretches of
2 ft 0 in gauge track is the line from Port
Elizabeth to Avontuur, 'dieselised' over a
large part of its route. Steam still works
from Assegaaibos to Avontuur using
German designed outside framed 2-6-2s

right
One of the South African 2 ft 0 in gauge
lines is the proud possessor of a 2-6-2 + 2-
6-2 Garratt painted blue. This engine,
cossetted by its driver, takes the daily
mixed train from Weenan to Estcourt. It
is now a tourist attraction at weekends

River, an hour or so's journey away, takes the trains past the perimeter of the game park and what could be better than a ride on the footplate of a 59 class with its huge train snaking behind it, watching out for giraffes, zebras and perhaps even the occasional lion. Somehow the old East African Railway system will not seem the same when the motive power on the trains is completely 'dieselised' and General Motors replace Beyer Peacock as locomotive manufacturers general to southern Africa. On the whole the steam fleet has stood up well to the onslaught of the diesel salesmen and lack of funds for diesel spares has tended to keep steam running. A great deal of activity can still be seen without going beyond Nairobi, which has the largest shed on the system. It has an allocation of fifty-seven steam locomotives of eight different types.

The world's least known stronghold of massive steam power is China, where steam is retained in accordance with a policy whereby this vast and rapidly developing country makes the most of its own natural resources. Today, especially in the north-eastern industrial areas, steam still reigns, not quite supreme but for China in equal partnership; diesel locomotives for the future are constructed side by side with equally modern steam locomotives. Huge freight trains of 3,000 tons in weight run steadily across the countryside over well laid and maintained track behind great mechanically-fired 2-10-2s, whilst modern 4-6-2s head inter-city passenger trains. Smaller but modern 2-8-2s of the *Aiming High* class were still being turned out of Tangshan works in 1976 whilst some huge 2-10-2s of the *Advance Forward* class were built as recently as 1975 and may still be in production at Tatung. In addition to the indigenous engines China still uses some American built shunters plus a number of ex-Russian 2-10-2s of class FD (originally *Felix Dzherzhinsky* class) supplied second-hand. Of the original class of some 3,200 built between 1931 and 1941 around 2,000 are thought to have been sold to China in the 1950s.

For those who are fortunate enough to be able to visit China, the country's railways provide a fascinating example of maximum use of indigenous resources and even more fascinating, no ban on railway photography – contrary to the usual attitude taken by Communist countries. Somewhat naturally the Chin-

South Africa also uses steam in abundance on its industrial lines, some of which are of considerable length. Most power is retired main-line locomotives and, painted red, green and blue, these look a fine sight at the head of their often very heavy trains

above
Coal from the Wankie Collieries is vital to the economy of several South African countries. The mines have their own fleet of steam locomotives in the form of 4-6-2s and 4-8-2s painted green. These work the traffic from the pithead to the main line at Thompson Junction

top
Branch-line traffic in Rhodesia is also Garratt hauled although usually by the smaller class, 2-6-2 + 2-6-2s

left
In spite of political difficulties traffic still flows over the Victoria Falls bridge between Zambia and Rhodesia. The motive power on the Rhodesian side is steam in the form of 4-8-2+2-8-4 or 4-6-4+4-6-4 Garratts

below
East African Railways, once a unified system linking Tanzania, Kenya and Uganda still uses steam although mainly on freights and on branch lines. All engines are painted red, including the huge 59 class 4-8-2+2-8-4s as well as the smaller 60 class of the same wheel arrangement. Nairobi shed, Kenya is host to both these classes, which, as do most EAR locomotives, carry Giesl Ejectors

China today is constructing modern diesel power to run side by side with its equally modern steam locomotives. Whilst many of the main passenger trains are diesel hauled, some from Peking's main station to Tientsin and the north east are hauled by *People* class Pacifics

ese do not really understand the Western craze of railway enthusiasm, but they do at least tolerate it. For the few groups able to gain entry to China, railways are there for travel purposes only and the enthusiast with his camera needs to be up betimes or be prepared to follow his hobby after the normal days educative work and sight seeing is complete. Chinese stations are not for loitering.

Technically it is still possible to take a train in Peking and end up in Moscow – indeed 'through' coaches operate on two routes, via Manchuria and via Mongolia, but for a Westerner this is a journey only to be made if perseverance is born in him. The Chinese section of the journey via Manchuria almost certainly still involves the constant sight of steam, with the 2-10-2s, 4-6-2s, 2-8-0s in profusion and wonderfully kept. The quicker Mongolian route is believed to be all-diesel, as is now the Russian portion of each route.

So Russia itself is no longer a haven of steam: various modernisation plans have been fulfilled and the *Russia* express, more popularly known as the Trans Siberian, is now steamless. Without doubt the highlight of the trip on the *Russia* in the last years was the 18 hours of steam haulage behind the magnificent P36 class 4-8-4s with the train rolling up hill and down at a steady 80 kmh the smoke seeming to be solid in the freezing atmosphere and the whole scene bathed in winter sunshine. Looking at their vast height of 17 feet one could well appreciate the truth that the Russian loading gauge is the largest in the world.

True, steam is about in the yards and on some of the branch lines, but it is only available to the determined and intrepid. Railway enthusiasm does not feature in the Intourist publications nor do the children's instructional 'pioneer' railways any longer even contemplate steam locomotives.

Steam for tomorrow

Until comparatively recently the idea of amateur enthusiasts taking over and operating a stretch of full-size railway would not have been a subject for serious contemplation; indeed, even 50 years ago few railways needed preserving. Today the fires of enthusiasm are burning fiercely in Europe, North America and Australasia, are beginning to take hold in Southern Africa and Asia and are starting to smoulder in South America. The almost unanswerable question is why? One reason could easily be that today people increasingly feel that they need to be involved in doing something creative. Nostalgia, of course, plays its part but anything as demanding and expensive as the preservation of railway engines and railways needs far more than dreaming of the past and wishful thinking to ensure success – or even their survival.

Long before the preservation of railways was to become an everyday fact the Bridgton & Harrison Railroad in Maine closed its doors. The scrapman however sold the locomotives to Ellis D. Attwood who made good use of them on his cranberry farm at South Carver, Mass. This is now the world famous Edaville Railroad

The first railway to be saved as an entity was the Talyllyn in North Wales. Reaching its centenary in 1965 it had been almost entirely refurbished and its two historic engines rebuilt

Although the first successful preserved railway to be opened for regular public traffic was in Wales, the credit for the earliest endeavours goes to the United States. North America was well endowed with short lines, branch lines and the narrow gauge; this was particularly the case in the states of Colorado and Maine – in the latter a network of 2 ft 0 in gauge railways existed until the 1930s. One of these, the Bridgton & Harrison Railroad, was near enough to the big towns of Boston and Worcester in Massachusetts to attract the interest of tourists and enthusiasts in its later days and abortive attempts were made to keep it going. When the line closed, the scrapman who purchased the assets became infected with the preservation bug and although the rails were sold in 1941, the locomotives and stock were laid on one side. These were purchased by an enthusiast, Ellis D. Attwood, for use on his cranberry farm at South Carver, Massachusetts. Interest in the line was such that the Edaville RR, as it is now called, became a major tourist attraction.

The first railway to be acquired *in situ* was in Britain – the then ageing and near derelict 2 ft 3 in gauge Talyllyn Railway in Wales, dating from 1865. At the time of its rescue in 1950, this delightful anachronism was the oldest surviving steam-hauled narrow-gauge passenger railway in the world. The story of its successful preservation, which led to imitation the world over, has been told too often to be repeated but the progenitors have good reason to feel pleased. Within a few years plans were in hand to resuscitate the historic Festiniog Railway further north, the pioneer line in the use of steam locomotives on so small a gauge. Fortunately for them, neither of the two new bodies formed to preserve the lines had to put down large sums of cash to purchase control – in fact the Talyllyn put down nothing at all. Both were also in recognised tourist areas where income could be reasonably assured. The other and very considerable advantage was that, being narrow gauge, the purchase and upkeep of locomotives and stock were within the limits of available finances. Success bred success and more Welsh lines were rescued or preserved.

These little trains have an ambience of their own; like all diminu-

tives, they appeal to the public and together with the beautiful countryside in which they work, this goes a long way towards ensuring their popularity. Proof enough comes in the form of visitors from countries and continents far apart; Australia, Southern Africa and North America as well as in Europe.

The next piece of serious preservation to follow the Talyllyn was on the other side of the world – in Australia. Here the Victoria Railways had, at one time, five 2 ft 6 in gauge feeder lines, one of these being close to Melbourne in the Dandenong Hills and at the end of a standard-gauge 5 ft 3 in suburban line; it thus had all the attributes of a successful tourist railway – narrow gauge (limiting cost), comparatively short trips (also limiting cost, but this time the customer's cost), excellent scenery and last but not least, easy access to a large centre of population. It greatly appealed to Australians, who flocked to ride behind the one original and two locally-built replicas of ancient Baldwin-designed 2-6-2 tanks and colloquially dubbed 'the Puffing Billy Railway'.

In 1953 a group of enthusiasts, learning that the Victoria Railways

intended to close because a landslip had occurred roughly half way along its tracks, persuaded the Railway's Authorities to maintain a weekend service over the truncated section. This ran from the end of the electrified suburban service out of Melbourne at Ferntree Gulley to Belgrave. To meet safety and union regulations on the one hand and save costs on the other, the Victoria Railways provided the train crews and enthusiasts did the rest. It proved a great success; so much so that when, seven years later, the VR decided to extend the suburban service further east over the route of *Puffing Billy's* line to Belgrave, enough money was found to re-open another 6·5 miles to the original terminus at Emerald, including clearing the landslip. The Puffing Billy Preservation Society can claim the credit for lighting another preservationist beacon and because patronage has been so great it has been able to restore a fourth locomotive in its Newport Workshops after the engine had been a static exhibit for some years. An added attraction on the Puffing Billy line is the Menzies Creek locomotive museum, containing among other treasures, an 0-4-2 rack-and-pinion

Further north at Porthmadog, the Festiniog Railway was also rescued from oblivion. This line was the first narrow-gauge railway in the world to use steam. It built its own unique double-Fairlie locomotives and today it is one of the leading tourist attractions in North Wales

Early preservation in Australia included the now well known *Puffing Billy Railway* from Ferntree Gulley near Melbourne. This 2 ft 6 in gauge line using Baldwin designed 2-6-2 tanks is jointly operated by Victoria Railways and enthusiasts

tank locomotive from Tasmania, a Heisler geared logging railway locomotive and a Beyer-Garratt.

The southern African enterprises include one in South Africa itself and one in Rhodesia. The former is not preservation *per se* but rather a response to public demand. This is the SAR 2 ft 0 in gauge line from Port Elizabeth to Loerie on the Avontuur line. The little train, headed by one of the NG 15 class 2-8-2s once used in South West Africa, takes passengers out towards the mountains most weekends. In Rhodesia preservation pure and simple, can be seen in the form of the Gwelo & District Light Railway, a 2 ft 0 in gauge line set up by enthusiasts on park land within the township of Gwelo, with locomotives once used on industrial work at Selukwe. Painted blue, these little trains, hauled by *Margaret* and *Buckeye,* give much pleasure at weekends and on special occasions for charities.

The outstanding American piece of 'preservation' is, as has been mentioned previously, the Silverton branch of the Denver & Rio Grande Western, on which many thousands of holidaymakers fill the twice daily trains out of Durango and where it is necessary, in the peak season, to reserve a seat up to *three weeks* in advance. Following this success a much longer section of the old D & RGW narrow gauge has also been acquired by the States of Colorado and New Mexico and now operates as a tourist railway. This Rio Grande spectacular is called the Cumbres and Toltec Scenic Railroad. For magnificent scenery and the sheer scale of its operation it is the equal of the Silverton train. By 1967 the last remnants of the D & RGW narrow-gauge empire (apart from the compulsorarily run Silverton train) had finished. Once the work of conveying materials for a natural gas plant at Farmington had been completed in the mid-1960s freight traffic diminished rapidly and during the whole of 1968 only five trains ran the 200 miles from Alamosa to Durango. With so little traffic closure was inevitable. Just before actual scrapping began the States of New Mexico and Colorado supported bills for a take over of the scenic section from Chama to Antonito, 64 miles of line together with nine locomotives and over 100 wagons (no coaches, since all these had been taken to Durango for the Silverton line). This truly magnificent railway climbs up to and over the Cumbres Pass, some 10,000 ft above sea level; the journey in converted box cars and wagons takes the best part of a day – the return trip by bus is accomplished in 75 minutes! Volunteers could not possibly run a public service on such a vast scale and a professional lessee was necessary; the line is now operated by Scenic Railways Inc of California. There are, of course, other American narrow-gauge lines in preservation, either operated as enthusiast enterprises or on a professional basis, such as the Edaville in New England and the East Broad Top in Pennsylvania but it would need another book to describe all of them.

A similar situation applies to Europe, where countries in the West have enthusiast-backed and operated lines, (in Eastern Europe Hungary has the Kastely Pioneer railway, which is certainly in the 'steam for pleasure' category). Sweden, France and Austria perhaps lead in preserved or surviving narrow-gauge steam, which can also be found in Holland where a little piece of the Rotterdam Steam Tramway has been kept.

The Swedish lines are all amateur-run and are fun. There are three: the Anten – Grafnas, about 30 miles north east of Gothenburg; the Jadraas – Tallas, to the north-east, close to Gavle and the East Sodermanlands Railway which is the real gem for enthusiasts. They are all delightful examples of preservation but the East Sodermanlands incorporates an unspoiled historic setting, 50 miles west of Stockholm, with a collection of representative rolling stock and equipment to show a minor Swedish Railway as it was.

France was one of the first countries to follow the successful Welsh narrow gauge re-openings and Wales can almost certainly claim to have fathered one of the finest lines in Europe – the Chemin de Fer du

Almost in the heart of Africa a 2 ft 0 in gauge steam railway has been built for love and pleasure – the Gwelo and District Light Railway in Rhodesia

Vivarais where Mallet tanks still run into the Massif. In the summer of 1968 Monsieur J. Arrivetz, already President of the little Meyzie line near Lyons, visited the Talyllyn and Festiniog Railways and was most impressed with what he saw. On his return to France he thought it might be possible, based on the information gleaned, to persuade the authorities to preserve and re-open a long section of this once huge and thriving network. Arrivetz and his friends argued for eight months, one of the best arguments being the provision of photographs of crowds boarding trains on the two Welsh lines. The ultimate effect was that the local authorities took over the 32 km long section from Tournon on the banks of the Rhone to the gastronomic town of Lamastre, in the foothills of the Ardeche. The Society now runs the line using some of the original Swiss-built o-6-6-o Mallet tanks for *les jours d'affluence* and railcars for the less busy times. There is usually a three hour break for lunch at Lamastre where at least one restaurant carries a high *Guide Michelin* recognition.

Austria built, and still operates, a large number of narrow-gauge systems. Few of these except the mountain rack railways and the Achenseebahn use one hundred per cent steam, but many have seen its attraction for the summer tourist and keep the necessary motive power in re-

serve for the tourist season. These include the Zillertal, Murtal and Styrian Local Government lines and most of these use the almost standard Austrian narrow-gauge engine, the outside-cylindered o-6-2T.

As a rule steam in Switzerland runs so that both profit and pleasure shall result; the only true preserved railway is the Chemin de Fer Touristique Blonay – Chamby., Here a steam service runs side by side with electric tramway stock for, like all good Swiss systems, this branch of the C de F Electriques Veveys, was completely electrified. Re-opened by the Society in 1968, it gives a 3 km ride over the metre gauge between the places of its title, taking passengers on a steeply-graded journey through woods and over an impressive viaduct high above Lake Geneva. One of the ambitions of the group is to provide a national narrow gauge railway museum on the line. To ride the system takes one back to the steam days of such exquisite lines as the Furka – Oberalp Bahn and the one-time Mittelbadische Eisenbahn of Germany (the Blonay – Chamby o-6-6-o Hanomag Mallet tank comes from the latter).

Preserved railways are not all narrow gauge, many in Europe and the United States use steam for pleasure over the tracks of now closed short or branch lines. In Great Britain and Europe these are

ususally run by enthusiasts looking for little return bar that required to maintain the line and its equipment, although even this becomes harder and harder as the inflationary spiral moves upwards.

Generally speaking the British lines are branches discarded by a retrenching national system. For example there is the Bluebell Railway in Sussex, the Dart Valley in Devon and the Severn Valley in Worcestershire. The lines acquired earlier, such as the Bluebell and the Worth Valley in Yorkshire, are short and controlled by enthusiast organisations, the others tend to be controlled by public companies. Somewhat naturally (other things being equal) the shorter the line the better its prospects for the costs increase with distance whilst revenue does not. The Dart Valley is an example. This company controls two lines, the Dart Valley Railway itself from Totnes to Ashburton and the Torbay Steam Railway from Paignton to Kingswear, both in the heart of excellent tourist country with a huge turnover of visitors each week during the season. Even so, in 1977 its Chairman found it necessary to send a begging letter to its shareholders admitting to a chronic cash flow problem. If this is so in such ideal circumstances, what of some others? The future is hazy and perhaps there are too many such railways for the public to support.

One of the longest and most spectacular narrow-gauge lines in the USA was the Denver and Rio Grande Western's route from Alamosa to Durango over the Cumbres Pass. A section of this route, between Chama to Antonito has been restored under the name of the Cumbres and Toltec Scenic Railroad using the original D & RGW locomotives

Preservation in Sweden includes the restoration of the Jadraas–Tallas Railway. This is all that is left of the 50 miles long Dela-Ockelbo-Norrsundet Railway, an industrial line in the north-east of the country

Let it be emphasied however, that a vast amount of work has been done by enthusiasts to preserve what they themselves feel worthwhile. It is to be hoped that this dedication, itself a product of a vital requirement in these days – job satisfaction – can be rewarded permanently by cost consciousness and efficient operation of the lines concerned.

In the United States the situation is somewhat different, so vast a country tends to localise attractions which in itself means that they have to be good, and to survive they have to make money. The annual Steam Directory of tourist railroads in North America contains around one hundred entries – a considerably lower number per head of the population than that of Britain.

American tourist lines, as with all others, depend for their success by being soundly situated in areas where the train itself is only a part of the attraction. Some American lines, in fact those which attract the most customers, form sections of amusement parks; outstanding amongst these are at Disneyland in California and the recently opened Disney World in Florida.

Like Great Britain and Europe America has mountain railways of which the Mount Washington Cog Railway is the oldest; it is worked by ancient, unique and attractive locomotives. This line is not technically a preserved railway but it is owned by

and run by a family which cares for it. A brand new steam locomotive to the design of the original 1870 engine has just been built. All are named; old No 1, a vertical boilered machine now on display at the lower terminus, is called *Old Peppersass*.

The premier standard-gauge lines include the Green Mountain Railroad in Vermont, New Hampshire which continues the business of being a freight carrier (with diesel) and runs steam tourist trains behind 1948-built Canadian Pacific Railway 4-6-2s. This is adjacent to the well known Steamtown Museum which was developed by F. Nelson Blount, who was unfortunately killed in an air accident before some of his considerable fortune could be spent on finishing the job. Another attractive and efficient line is the Strasburg Railroad 65 miles west of Philadelphia. Obeying all the set rules it is only 4·5 miles long, close to a large centre of population, is in a very touristy Dutch country area and has adjacent to it the Railroad Museum of Pennsylvania. It is one of the oldest and busiest tourist lines in the USA.

An unusal line south west of Washington DC in West Virginia is the Cass Scenic Railroad. Here 11 miles of standard-gauge track once used as a logging railway climb a steeply graded route which includes switchbacks, sometimes at gradients of 1 in 8. Originally serving vast

above
Another piece of branch line run by enthusiasts is the section of the Great Western's Severn Valley Railway between Bridgnorth and Bewdley. This is Britain's longest stretch of tourist railway

above, left
One of the most important of the railways in Western Europe to be rescued is the C de F du Vivarais in the Massif Central of France. This mountainous line using 0-6-6-0 Mallet tanks now has two sections running, the main piece being from Tournon to Lamastre

right
The first standard-gauge line in Britain to be taken over and run by enthusiasts was the old Southern Railway branch from Horsted Keynes to Sheffield Park in Sussex. Using largely engines once common in the south of England, it is a first class working museum

areas of Federal Government owned forest on the southern side of Cheat Mountain, the logging run closed in 1960. Due to the persistance of a devoted rail fan called Russell Baum, the State of West Virginia was persuaded to purchase the geared engines of the famous design conceived by the Michigan inventor Ephraim Shay, plus some of the rolling stock with the intention of keeping the system as a tourist attraction. It was re-opened in 1964 and today tens of thousands of tourists travel long distances to ride with the Shays to the top of Bald Nob, a return trip of 22 miles which takes 4½ hours. Moreover, the re-opening of the railroad has made the whole town of Cass come to life again and a piece of yesterday has

been kept for today. Even more unusual for America is the fact that it was State enterprise which saved the day.

In Europe the majority of standard-gauge tourist lines, although operated by preservation societies, still belong to national railway networks; these are usually disused or carry very little normal traffic. Examples are the Chinon–Richelieu line in France and the Hoorn to Medemblik branch of the Dutch State Railways. The French scheme, well organised and gently rustic, uses pleasing pieces of ancient 2-6-0 machinery to take its passengers at a leisurely pace through the Chateau country. The Dutch think more in terms of the light railway or tramway, and their pro-

above
Britain is fortunate in having a magnificent National Railway Museum. From time to time certain of its exhibits are lent to responsible preservationists. One of these, Great Northern Railway 4-4-2 No 990 is at Oxenhope on the Keithley & Worth Valley tourist railway

right
To ensure success, preserved or tourist railways need to be attractive to intending visitors or in the heart of already existing attractions. Such lines exist at Disneyland in the USA and, as seen here, at Knotts Berry Farm, Buena Park, California

jects are some of the few examples of this form of preservation in the world. Holland was one of the first European countries to dispense with steam traction and their last operable locomotive, a Beyer Peacock 4-6-0 which was retired to the Utrecht Railway Museum in 1956, is now occasionally steamed for enthusiasts. A decade later a further closure was being contemplated, that of the Rotterdam Steam Tramway which ran an effective suburban service out to Hellevoetsluis. This was rapidly becoming an anachronism although it had reserved tracks which ran away from the road over most of the journey out of the city centre limits. Its ancient steam locomotives had been all but retired but the elderly internal-combustion locomotives and permanent way would soon have needed replacement. In the event the RTM lasted into the mid 1960s and the Tramway Stichting trust was formed with the initial object of saving this equipment. A short section was later preserved at Hellevoetsluis but a unique opportunity came in 1968 when the State Railways freight branch from Hoorn to Medemblik, north of Amsterdam, was 'taken over'. This was in an established tourist area and

One of France's pleasant branches to be used by preservationists is that from Chinon to Richelieu in the Chateau country. Motive power is an old 2-6-0

there was adequate covered accommodation at Hoorn to serve as a depot and workshop.

In the early days the Dutch State Railways provided the drivers and the Trust used hired coaches but as time went on confidence was established all round and an operating organisation called Stoomtram Hoorn–Medemblik BV was set up. Ancient tramway-type locomotives were obtained, including a 1921 0-4-0 Henschel built for the Gooishe Tramway and rescued from a sugar factory and a former metre-gauge Belgian locomotive from the Chemins de Fer de L'Artois. The Stoomtram Hoorn–Medemblik BV now runs a regular timetabled service, plus some freight, and this short line running as it does between two pleasant market towns is as near to a living museum as one might ask.

The success of the TS at Hoorn gave the preservationists a further inspiration and with the co-operation of the State Railways two other freight only branches offer the attraction of privately owned steam excursion trains. One is at Goes in the south west of Holland on the island of Zuid – Bevland and the other near to the German border at Enschede.

The Cass Scenic Railroad is a one time logging line in West Virginia. It is a great tourist attraction and uses geared locomotives in the form of Shays and a Heisler for its motive power

left
In New Zealand the state also thinks
progressively towards preserved steam,
exemplified by the running of the
Kingston Flyer between Lumsden and
Kingston in the South Island. The
locomotives used are those which ran the
branch in days of steam, the Ab Pacifics.

below
The French also have their standard-
gauge museum pieces and a National
Railway Museum. One of the treasures is
a Crampton single-wheeler once
belonging to the Paris–Strasbourg
Railway

above
In Holland there is a first class system of
co-operation between the State Railway
and preservationists. One such example is
the Tramway Stichting Trust which
operates the branch line from Hoorn to
Medemblik

The fact that preserved steam is still alive in the USA was amply demonstrated by the Freedom Train – a National travelling exhibition which covered the USA during 1976 and 1977

The Dutch authorities have also used their restored 4-6-0 No 3737 for steam excursions from time to time and very fine she looks in her shining green and polished brass. Fortunately the running of old express locomotives over the tracks of their heyday is not confined to Holland alone; surviving engines are run in many countries which have dispensed with steam. Some are maintained by their original owners, that is the railway organisations themselves, and brought out for an occasional airing, this happens in

Canada, the USA and to a more limited extent in Europe and Australasia. In New Zealand, for example, the Government Railways now have the *Kingston Flyer,* a vintage steam train which runs between Lumsden and Kingston, South Island. In the days of steam New Zealand had just about everything a railway enthusiast could want, hard working, steeply-graded lines in dramatic scenery and big modern locomotives but no shortage of old warriors either. The *Kingston Flyer* uses restored coaches

dating from the turn of the century and two of the handsome Ab class Pacifics which were taken out of the scrap yards and overhauled. The Flyer now runs twice daily, including Sundays, during the whole summer season from Christmas to Easter, taking only 80 minutes for the 38 miles with eight stops and sharp climbs over two summits. Private preservation of course, also exists in New Zealand and the NZR co-operates by allowing these locomotives to run over their tracks with main-line steam excursions.

The Americans, too, adopt this system with the D & RGW operating their Silverton train and, *mirabile dictu* the Union Pacific keeping their huge and modern 4-8-4 No 8444 solely for fan trips, as does Canadian National with a 4-8-2. To see these giants at the head of their long trains blasting their way across the countryside is to have a glimpse of the glory of North America's railroading.

The fact that preserved steam is still alive in America was amply demonstrated when the 1976 Bi-

Southern Pacific 4-8-4 No 4449 takes the Freedom train through Bakersfield, California, a few minutes before dawn on 22 December 1975

centennial was celebrated with a nationwide tour of the steam hauled American Freedom Train. The locomotives which headed it included AFT No 1, formerly Reading 2101, a 4-8-4 which contains boiler sections from a 2-8-0; AFT No 4449, Southern Pacific GS 4-8-4, built at Lima; and AFT No 610, a Texas & Pacific 2-10-4, also Lima product.

In Britain the situation is different in that the nationalised British Railways were so anxious to put on a *new look* and to be, in their terms, *forward thinking* that steam departed in a holocaust. Because of this, during the period between 1967 and 1973 no railway officer dared show any form of enthusiasm for working museum steam nor be seen to be giving help to the enthusiast cause. In consequence British Railways kept nothing which they intended to operate as preserved steam – it was left to private enterprise. In the event several steam centres were set up, mostly on the sites of disused motive power depots.

So steam centres such as those at Birmingham, Carnforth (Lancs), Didcot (Berks), Dinting (Derbyshire) and Hereford came into being and can now house the majority of the colourful British express and mixed traffic locomotives which were saved privately from the breakers torch. These centres regard themselves as working museums and some have gone to the trouble to ensure that they provide the necessary museum-piece machinery to keep their charges fit for work. Fortunately, British Railways have in recent years seen fit grudgingly to allow a limited number of steam excursions on to their tracks at charter rates considerably above

right
One of Britain's most famous express engines No 4079 *Pendennis Castle* a record breaker of 1925, was sold to a railway in Australia in 1977. Australia's gain was very much Britain's loss

below
Ireland too has its preserved steam operating over main-line tracks. Engines include the Great Northern 4-4-0 *Slieve Gullion,* resplendent in sky blue and scarlet

those they would charge for their own diesel or electrically hauled trains. An undertaking has been given that these arrangements will continue until 1979 but beyond then there is a question mark. Steam excursions were originally inaugurated for the enthusiast who wanted to travel behind express engines at speed but rail fans are limited in numbers and there is a risk that the market has become saturated at the high prices charged. There is also the escalating cost of repairs and renewals to be considered. Sadly not everyone is always altruistic and already one of Britain's most notable pieces of railway heritage No 4079 *Pendennis Castle* has been sold to Australia for a very considerable sum.

Index